Mandalas in Glorious Color

Book 14
Mandalas for Crafting and Art

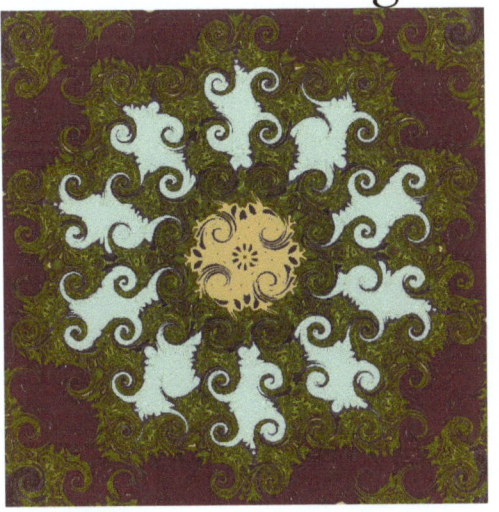

GRACE BRANNIGAN

Designed by Elaine Warfield

Art in Color Series
Mandalas in Glorious Color
(Mandalas for Crafting and Art)
Book 1 through Book 20

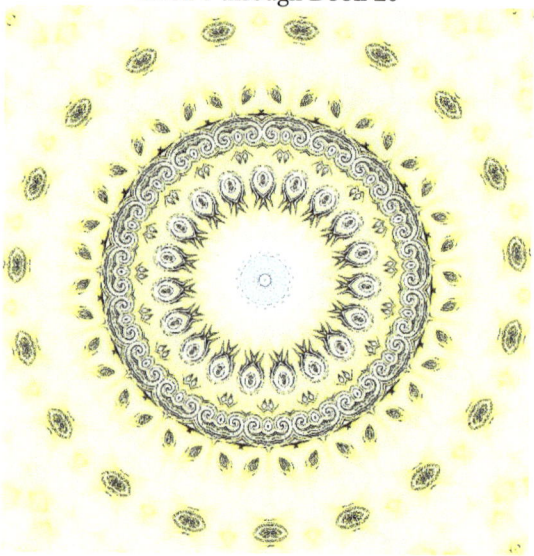

Author Website: http://www.GraceBrannigan.com
Mandalas in Glorious Color Book 14
by Grace Brannigan
Designs by Elaine Warfield
Copyright 2015 Elaine Warfield
ISBN-13:978-1514799420
ISBN-10:1514799421

License Notes

Questor Books, P.O. Box 100, East Jewett, New York, 12424 USA

Mandalas are spiritual and ritual symbols representing the universe. They may be used for focusing attention, as a spiritual guidance tool and also for establishing a sacred space. Some people like to use them in meditation practices.

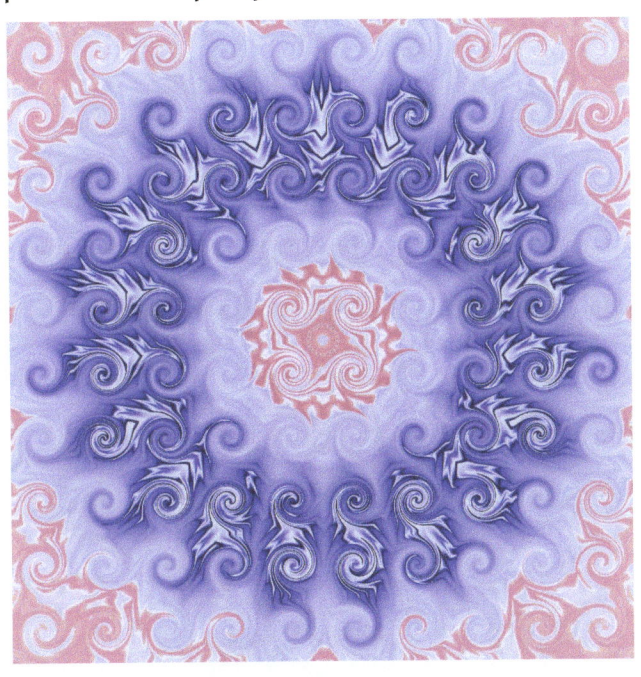

Whatever your preference, please enjoy these visually appealing, full-color Mandalas.

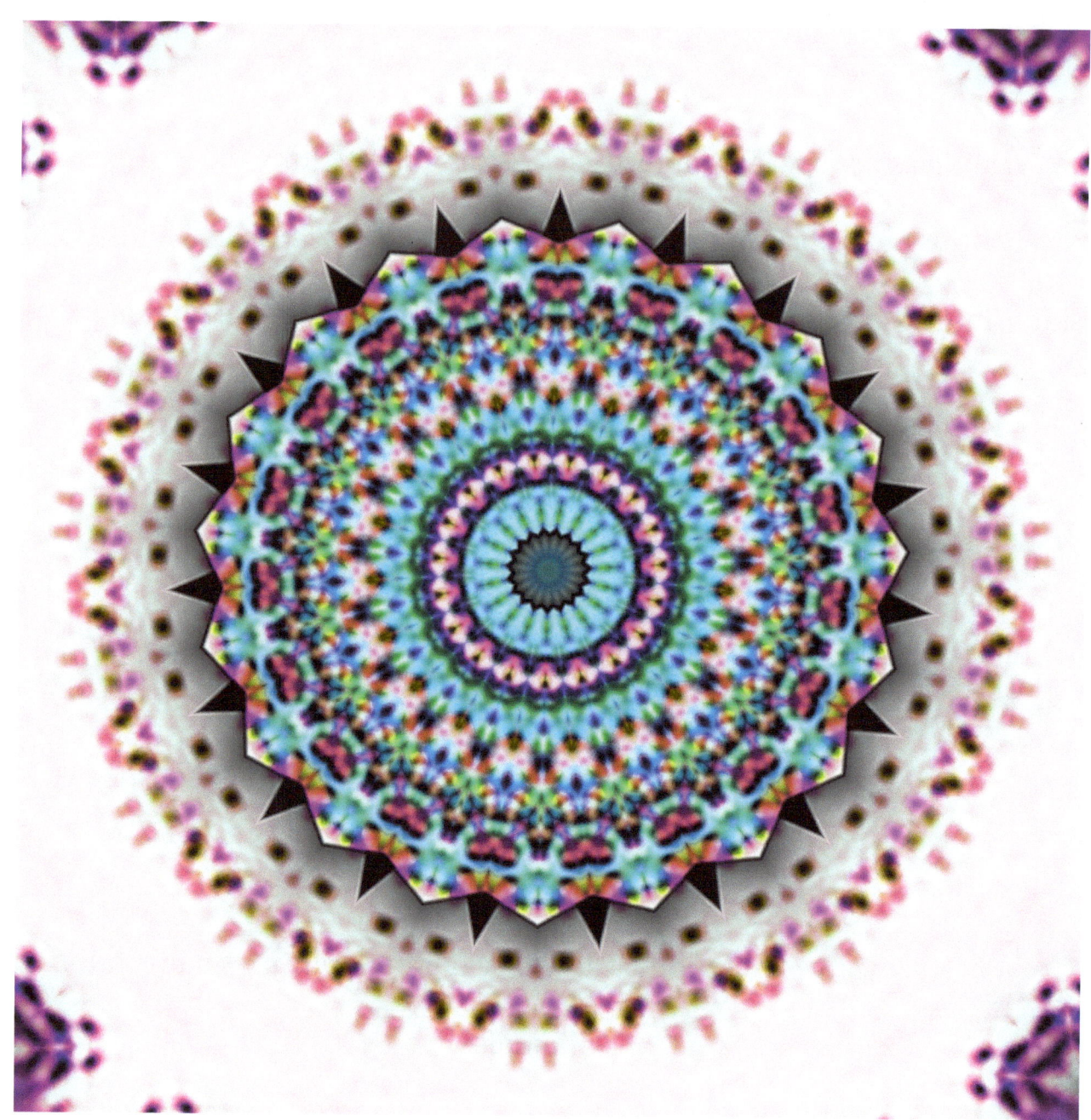

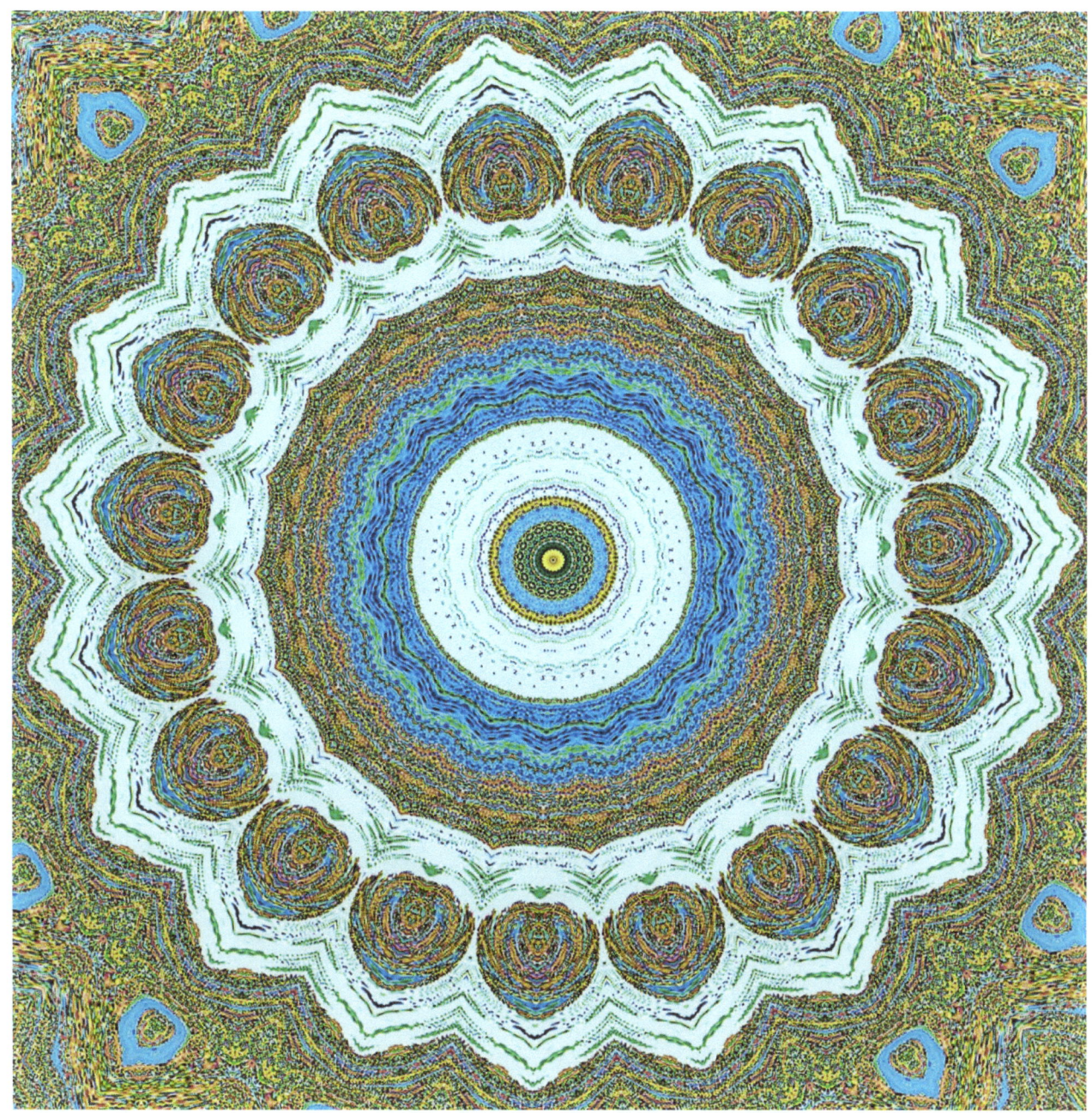

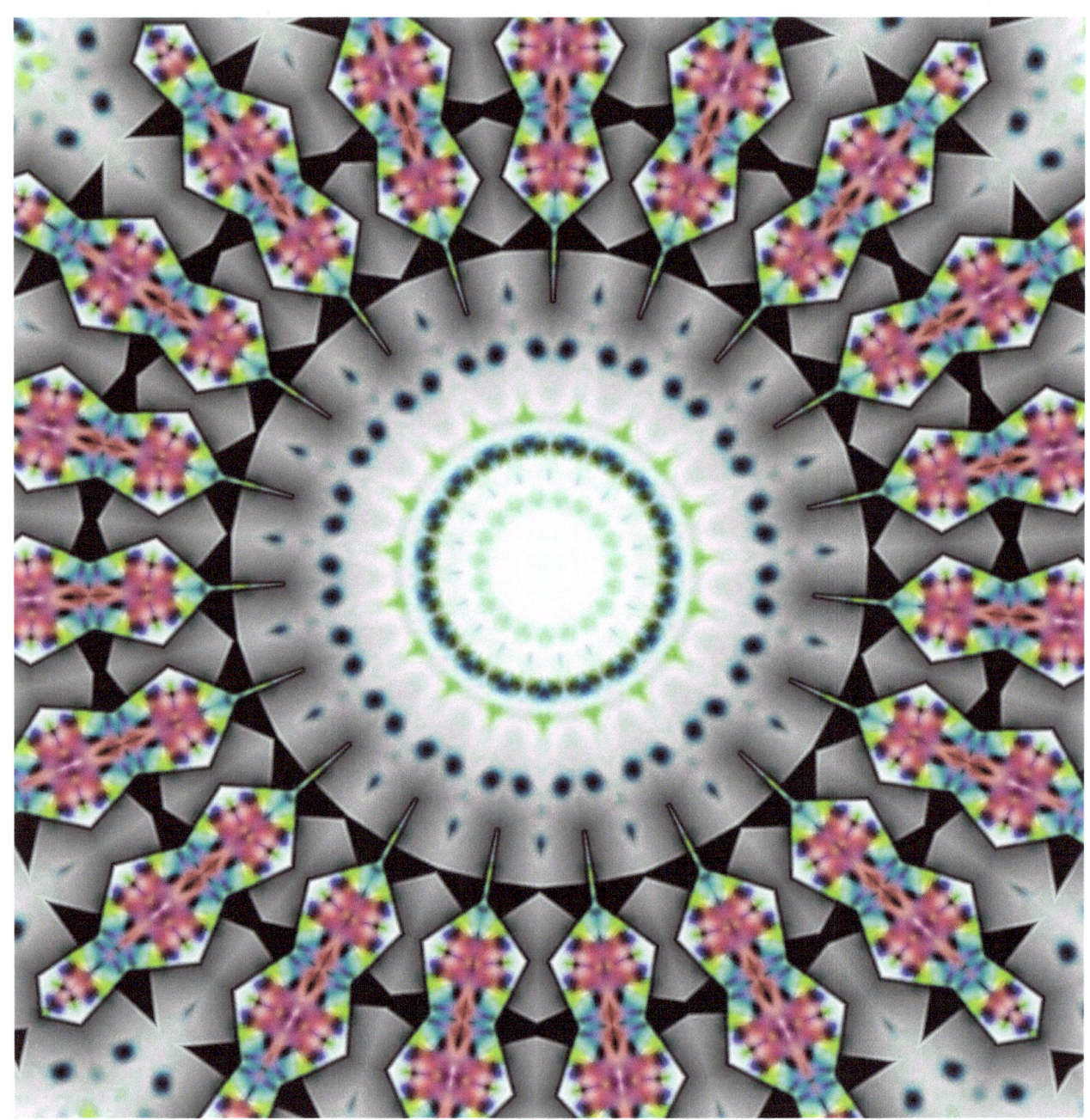

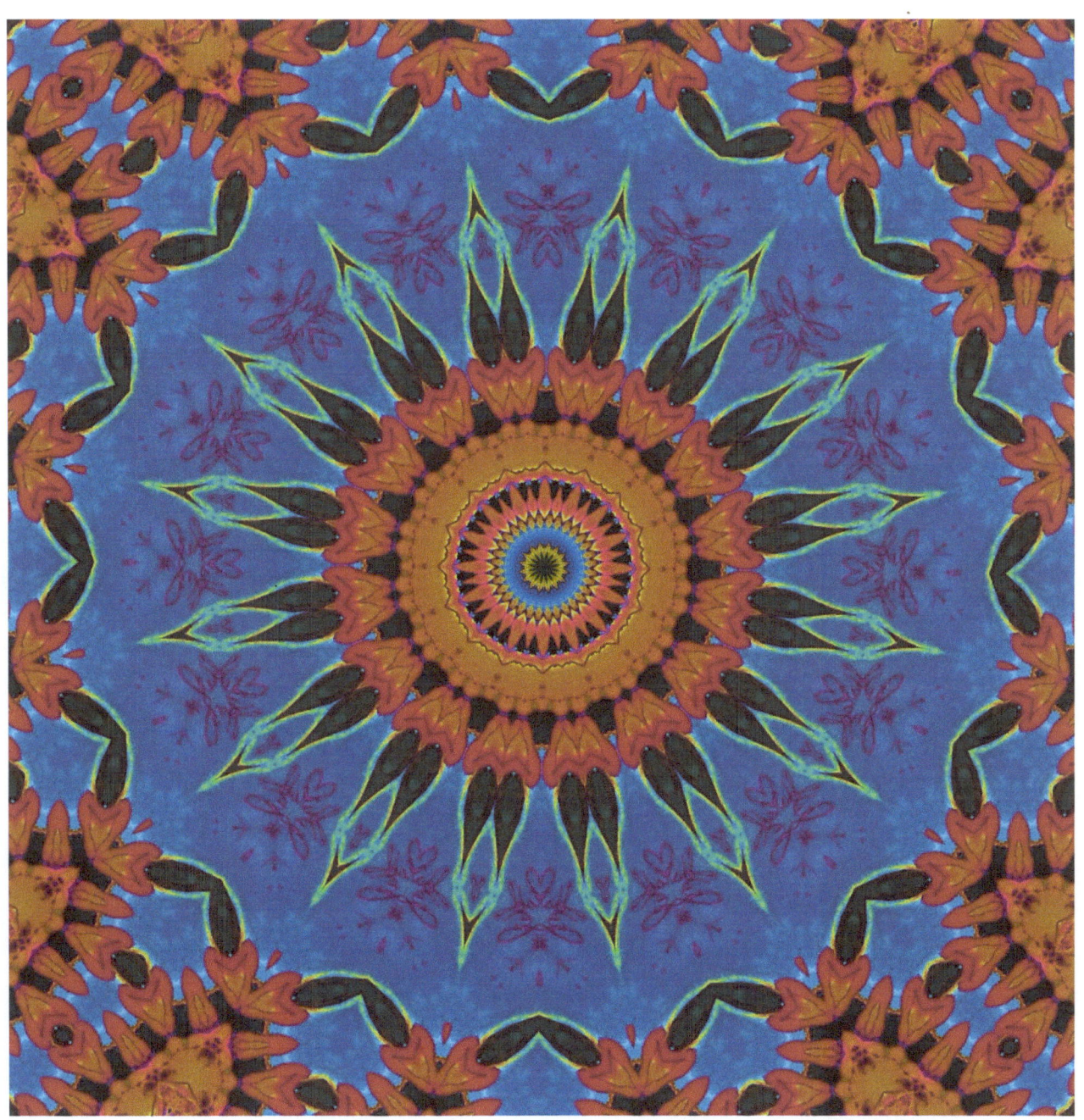

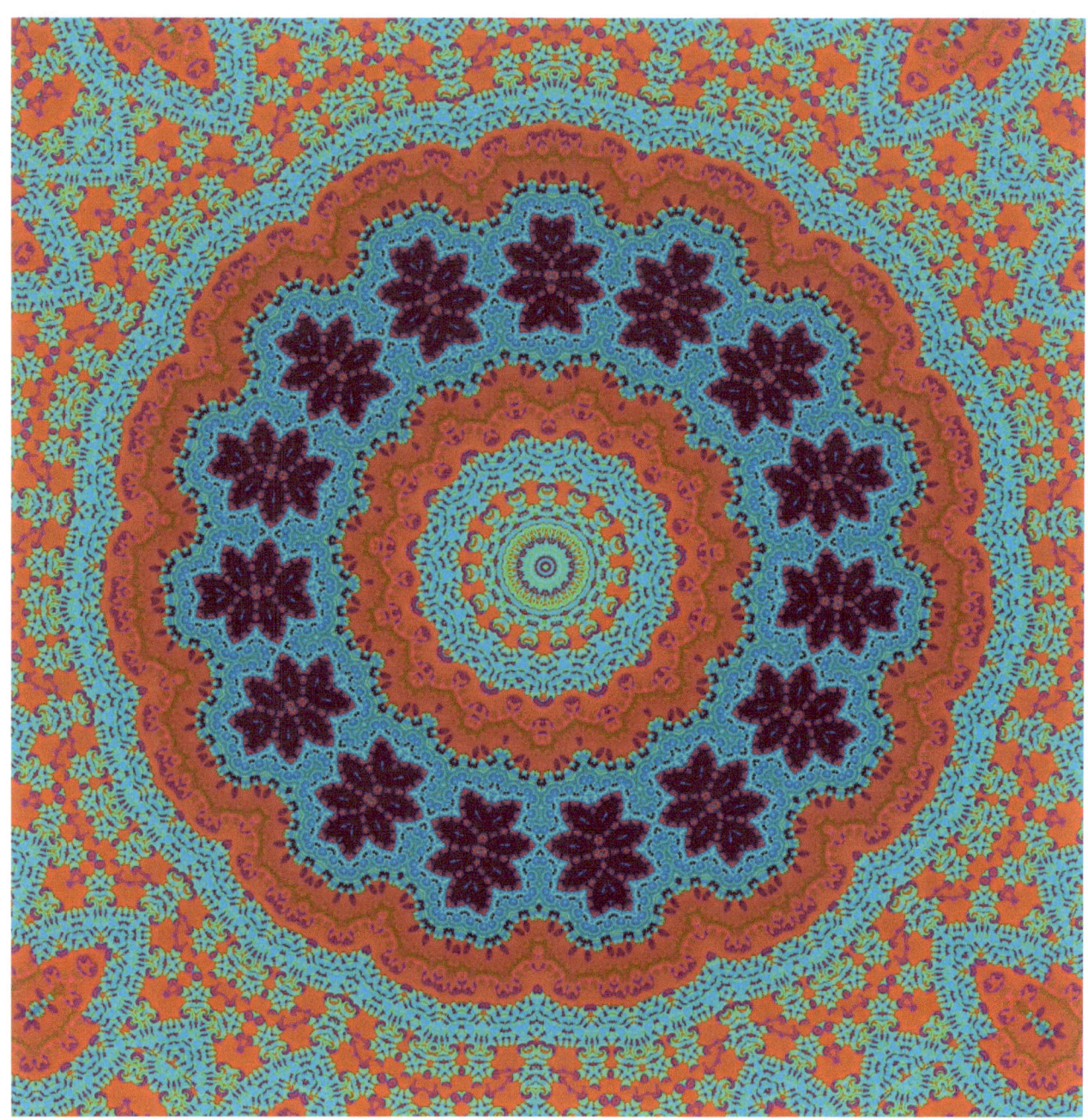

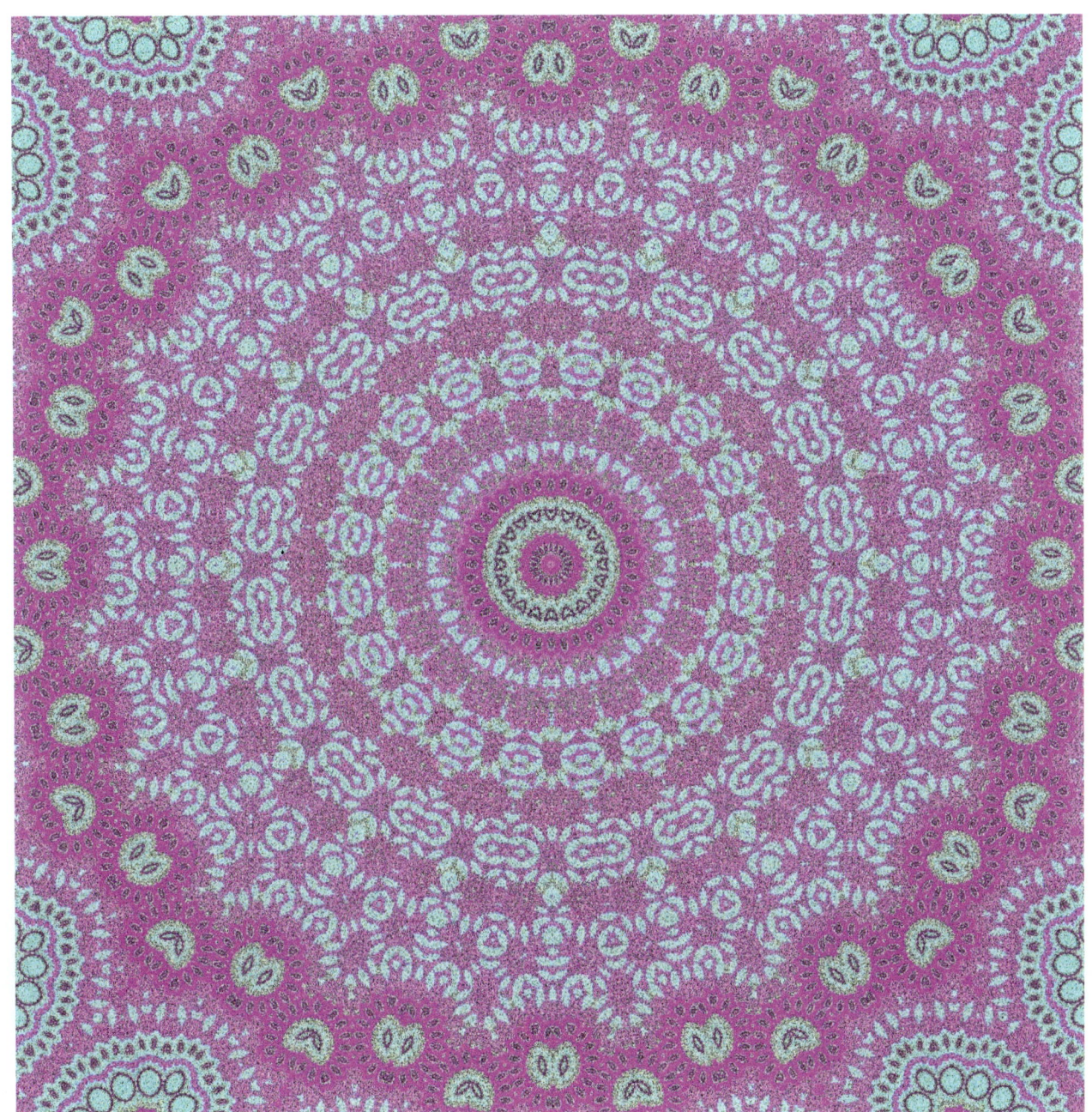

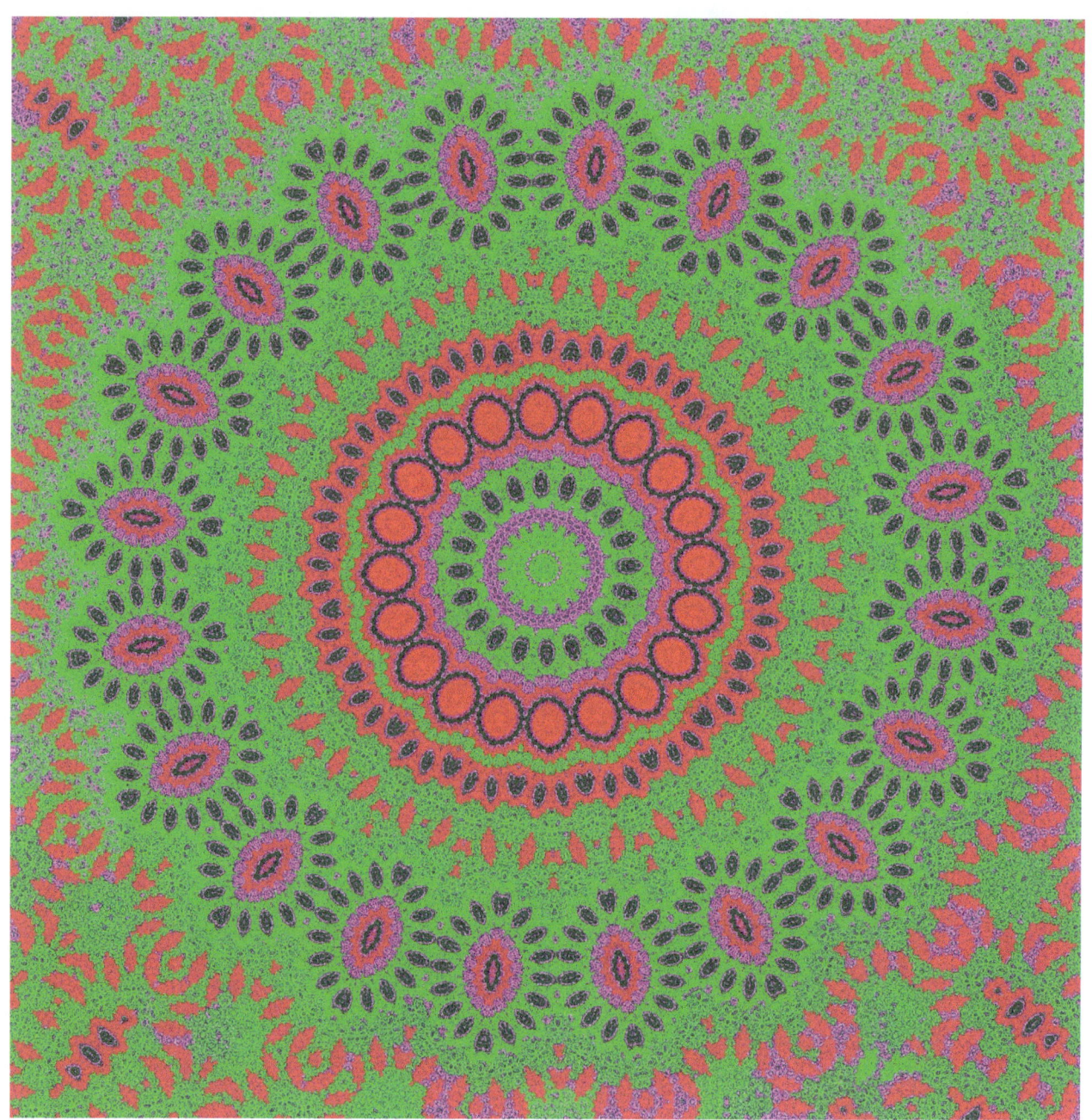

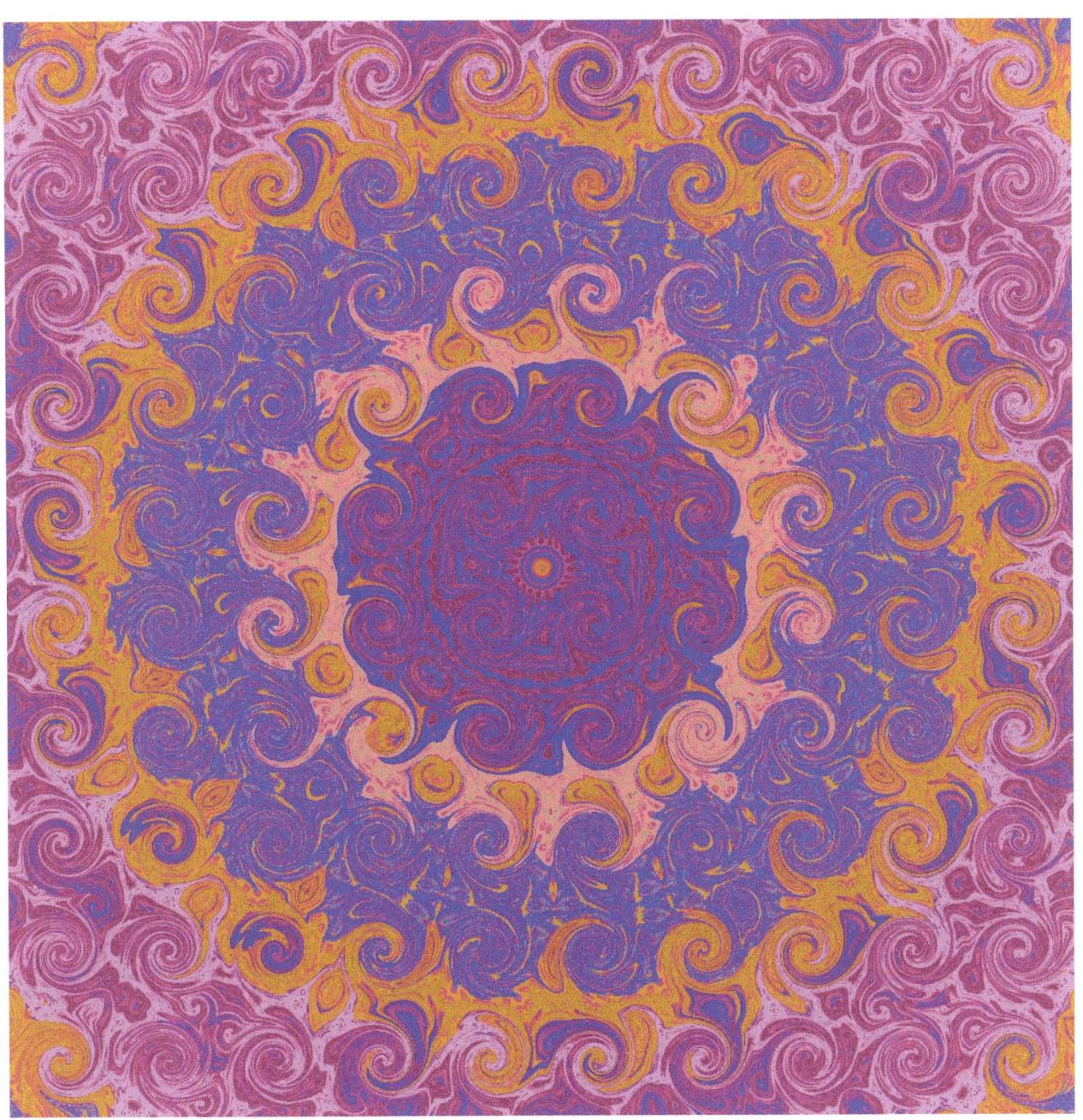

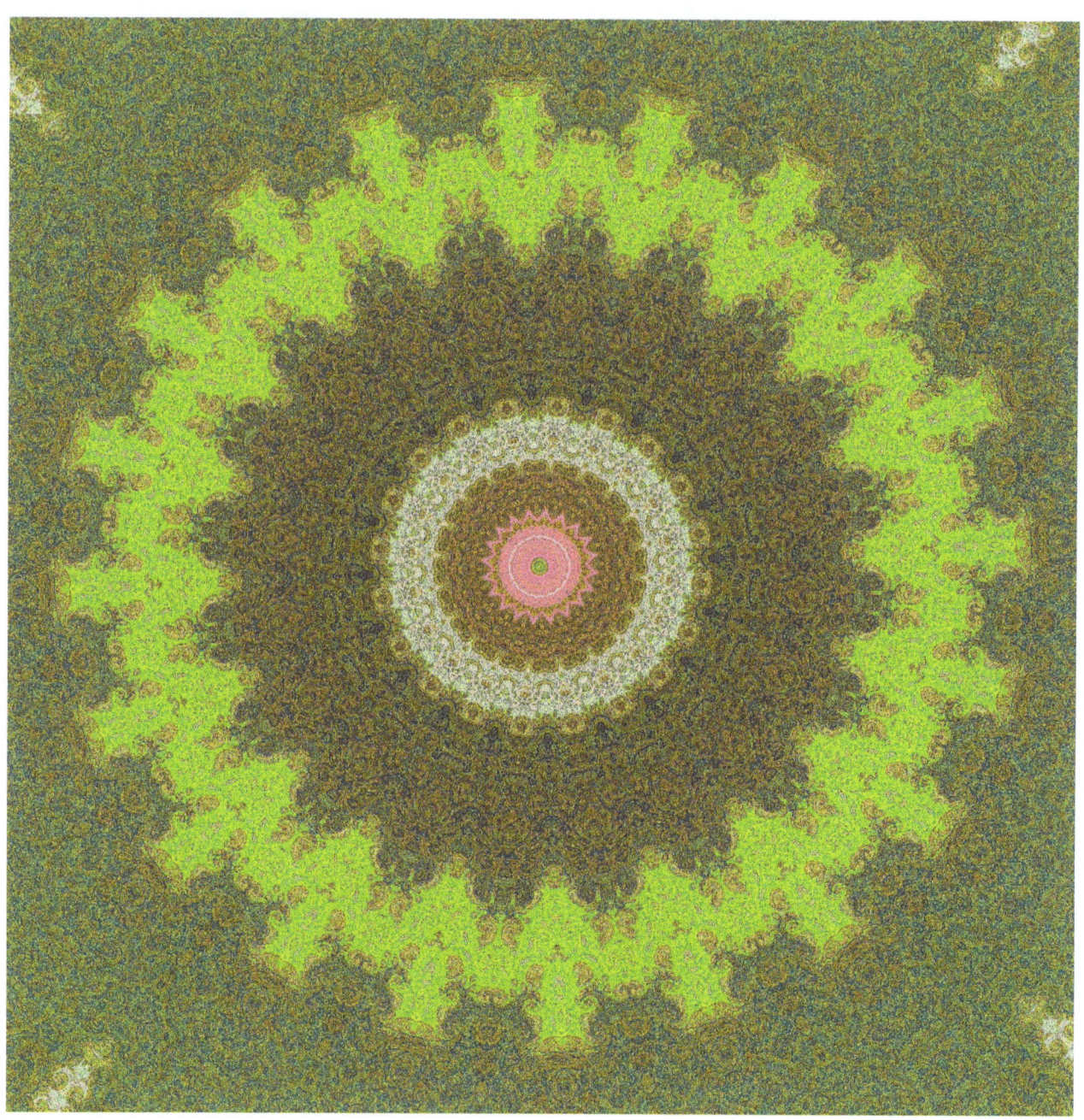

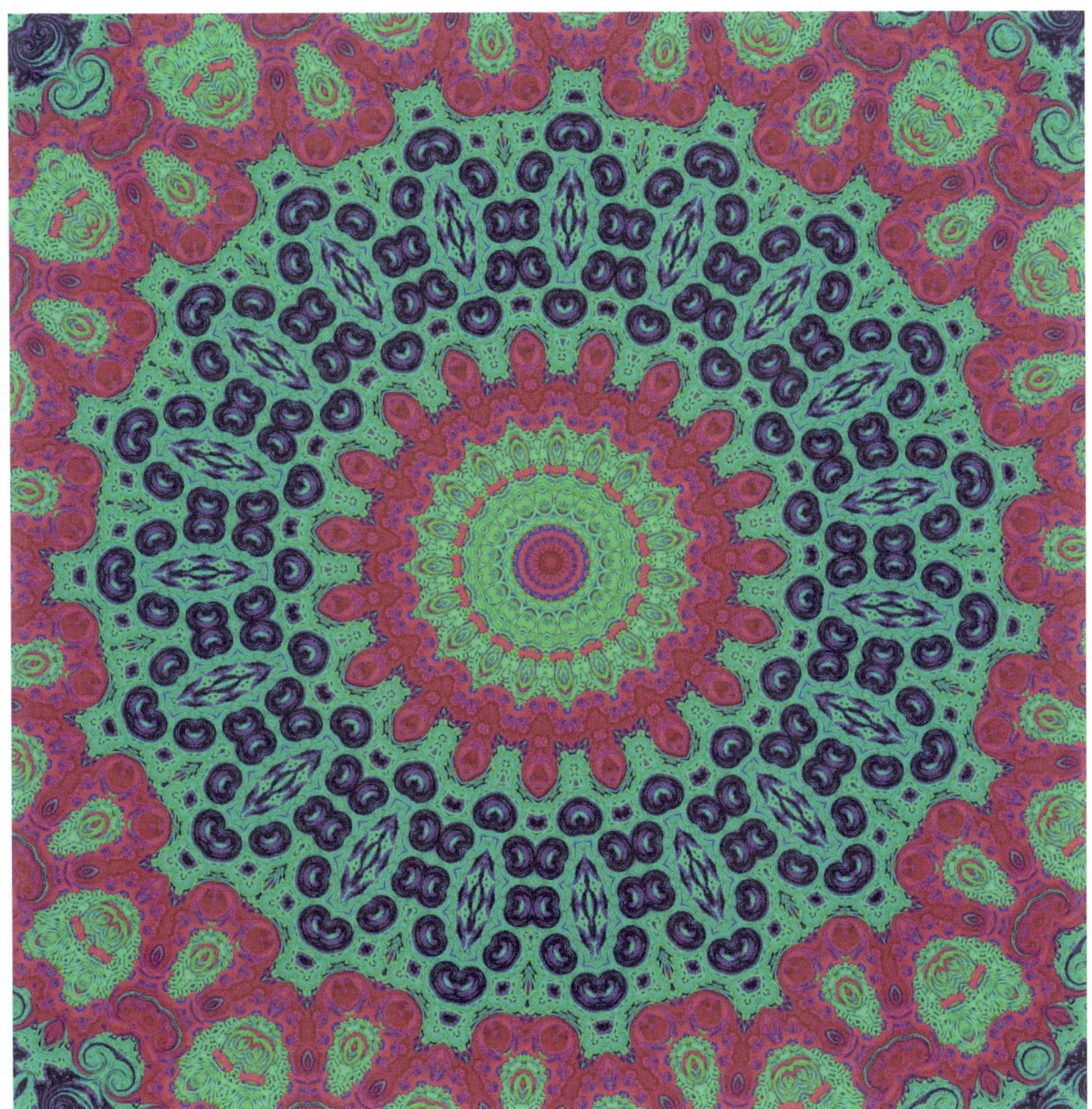

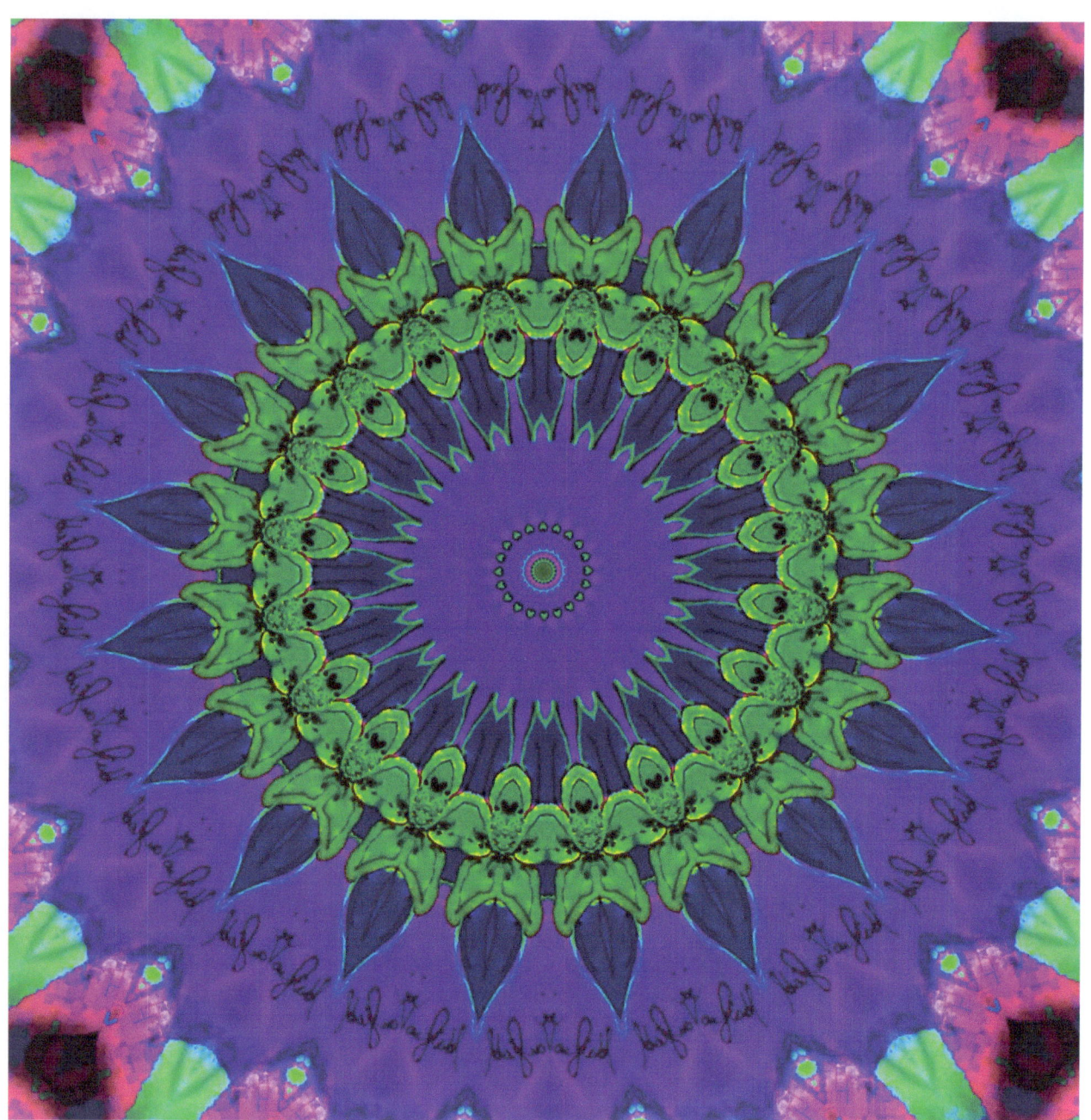

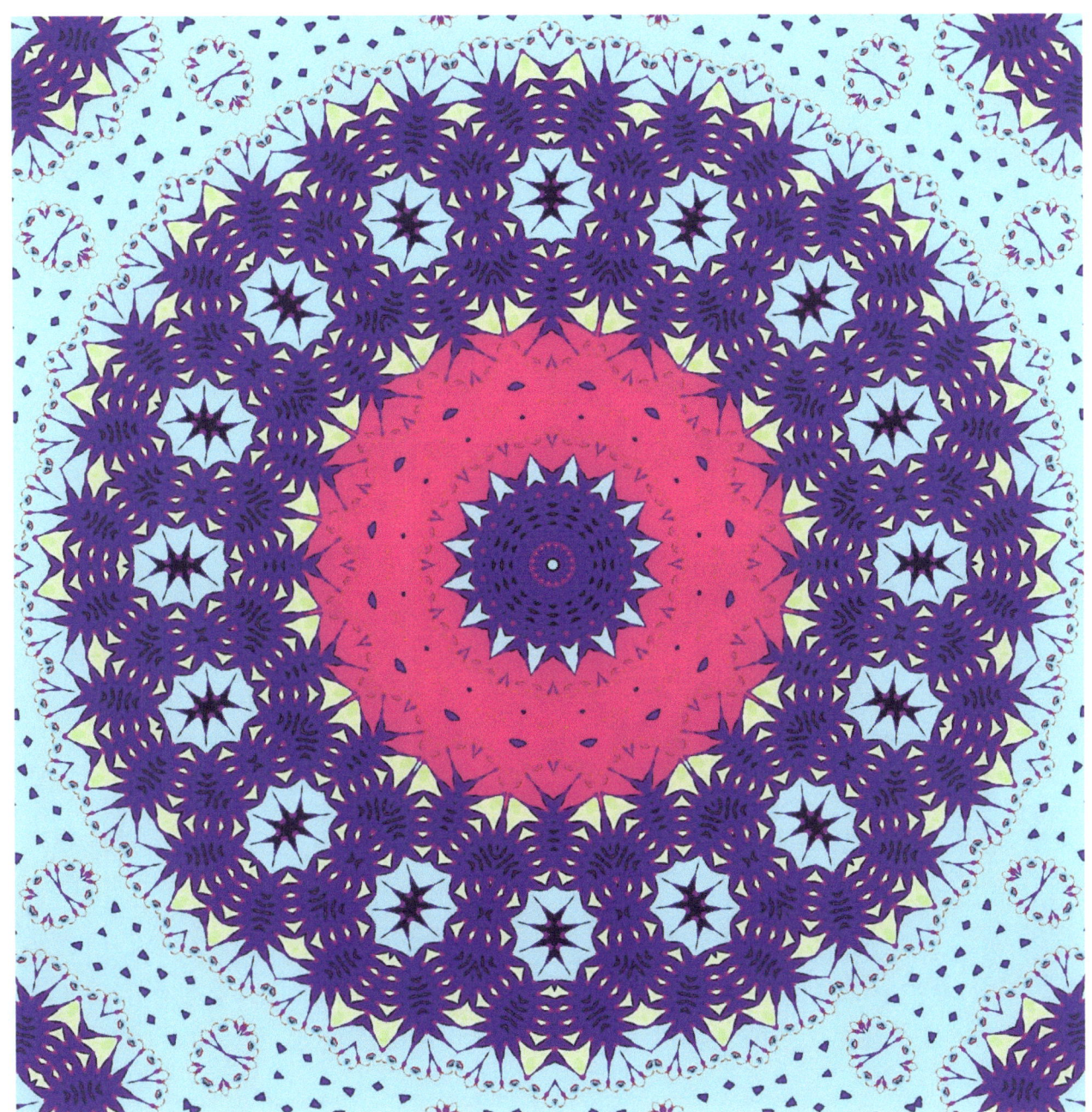

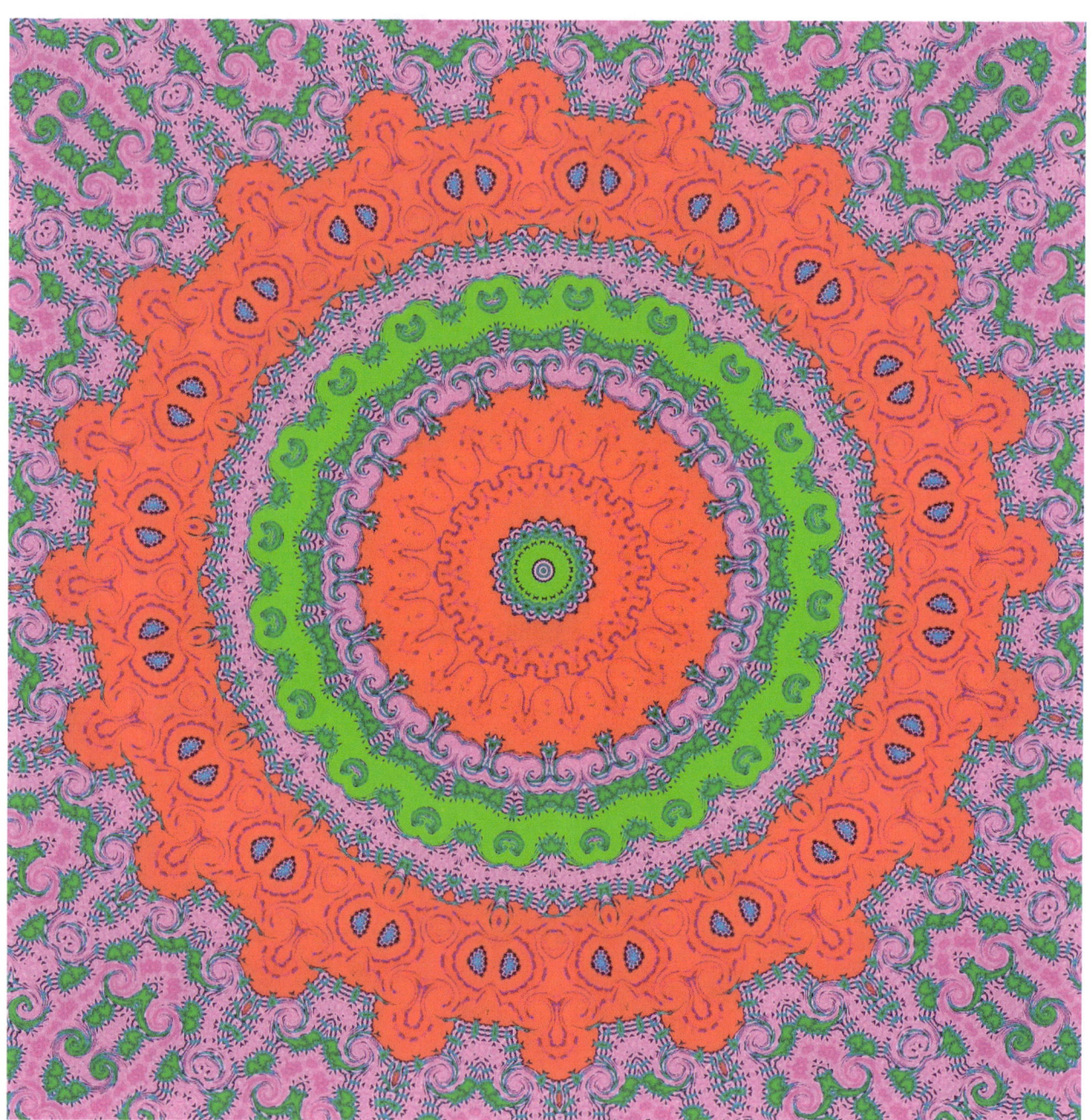

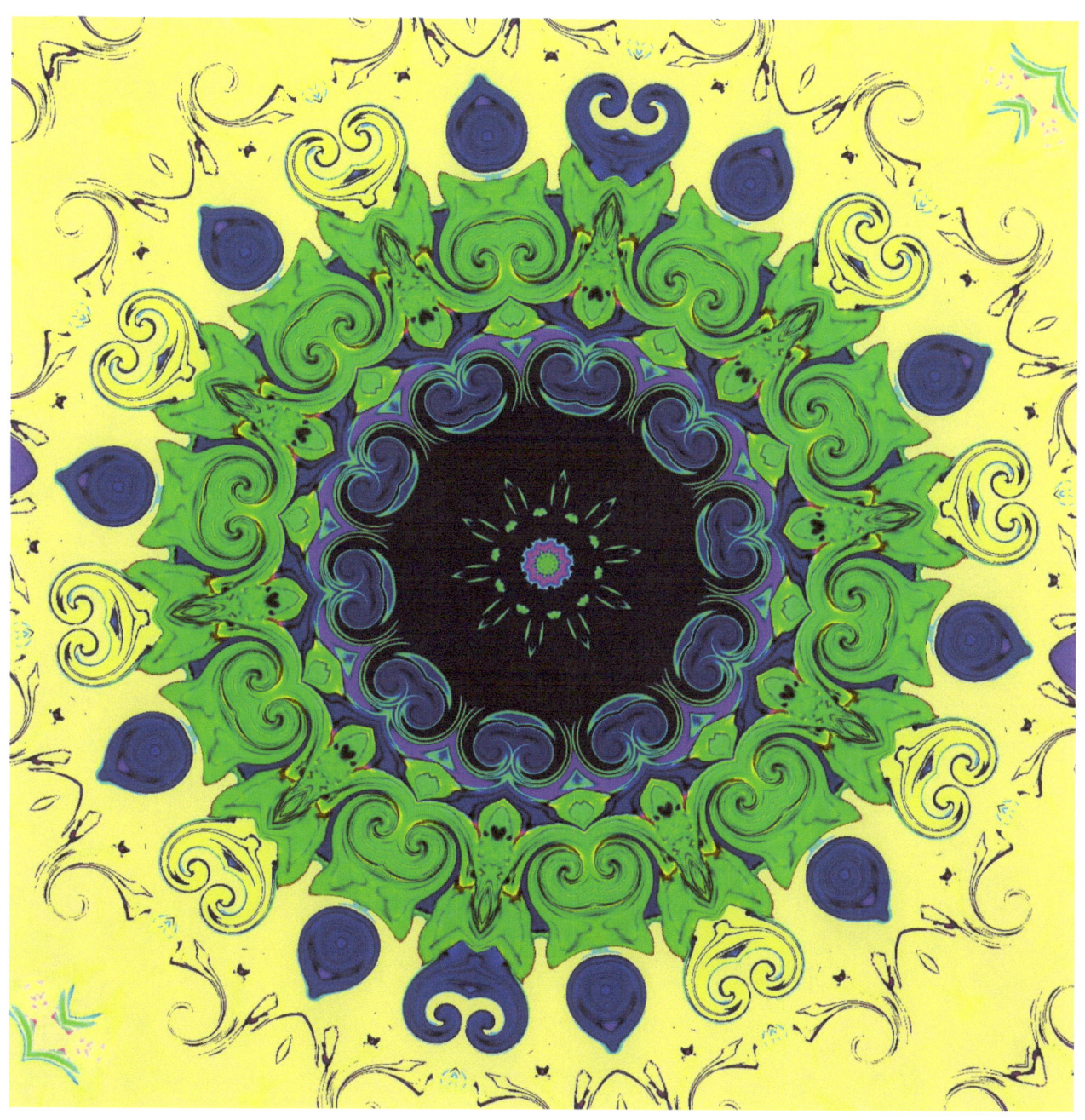

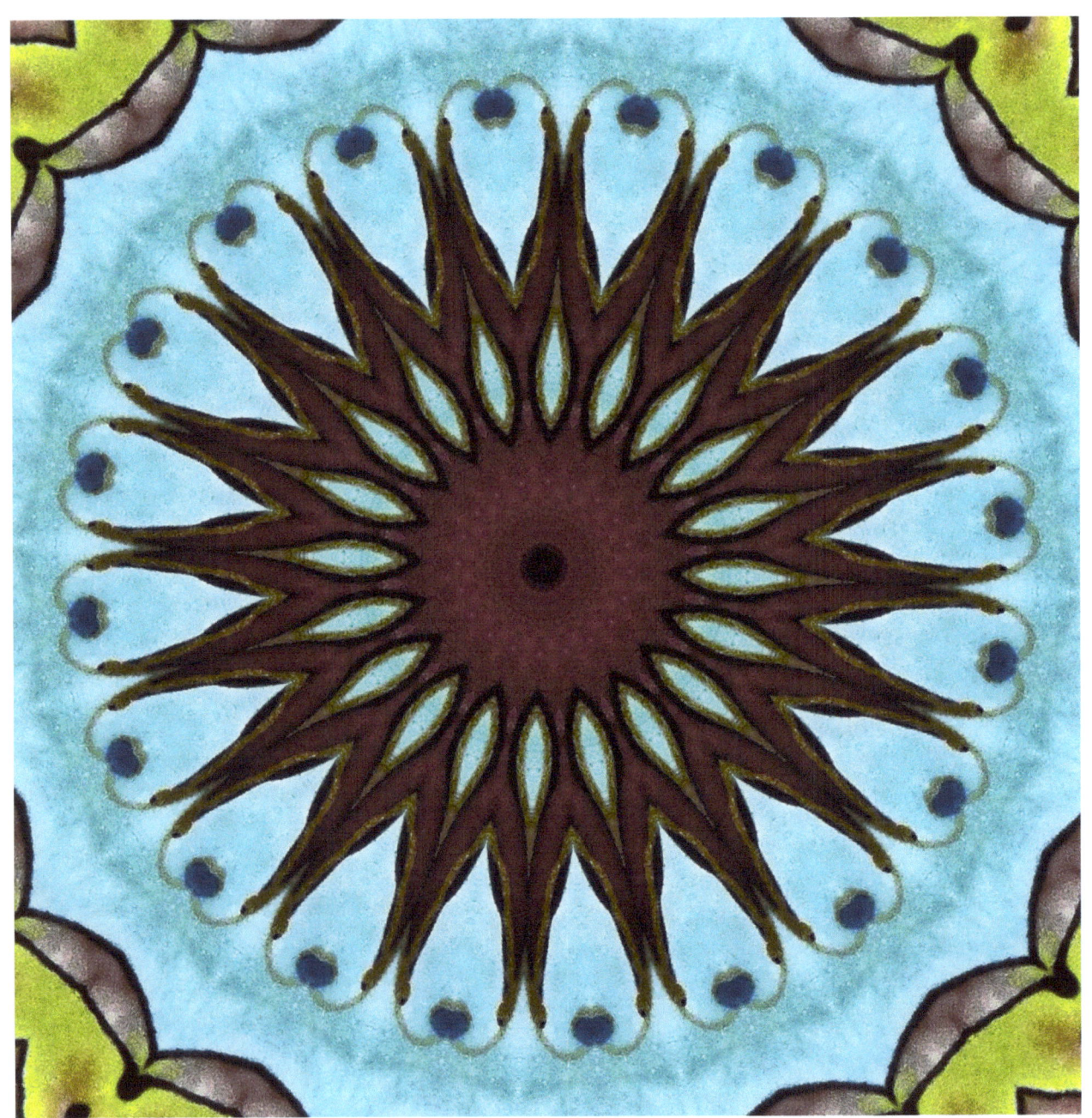

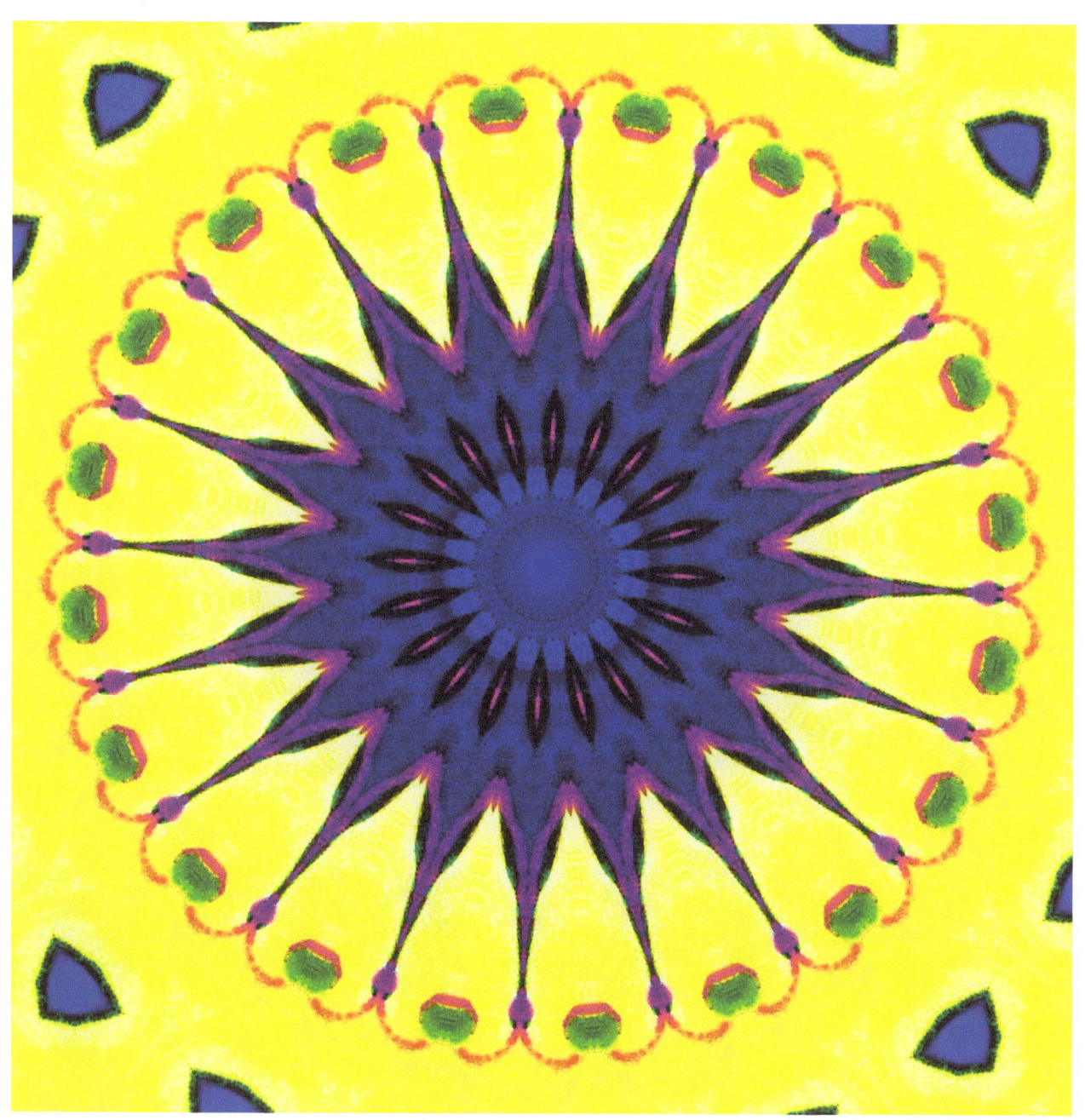

19

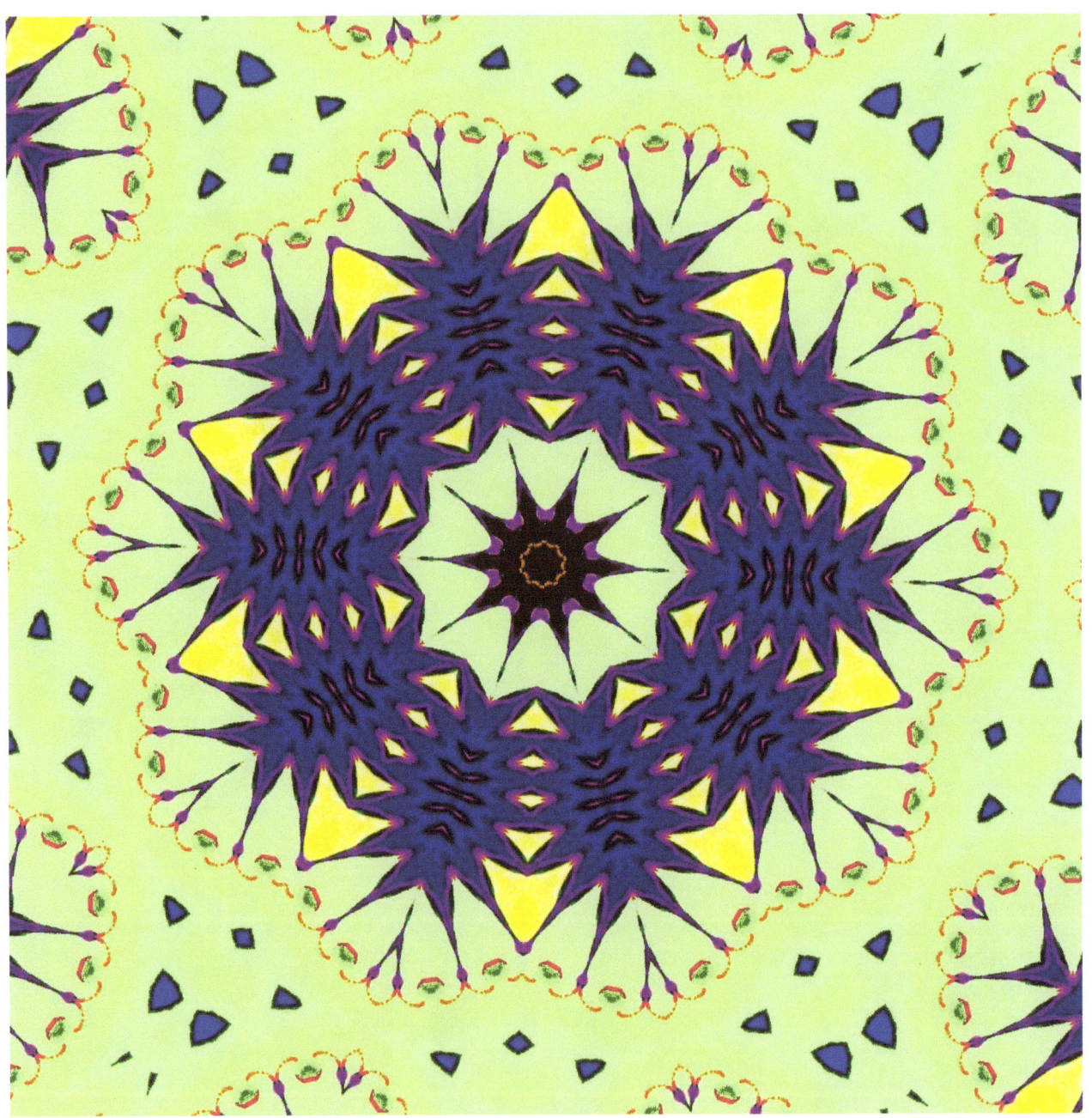

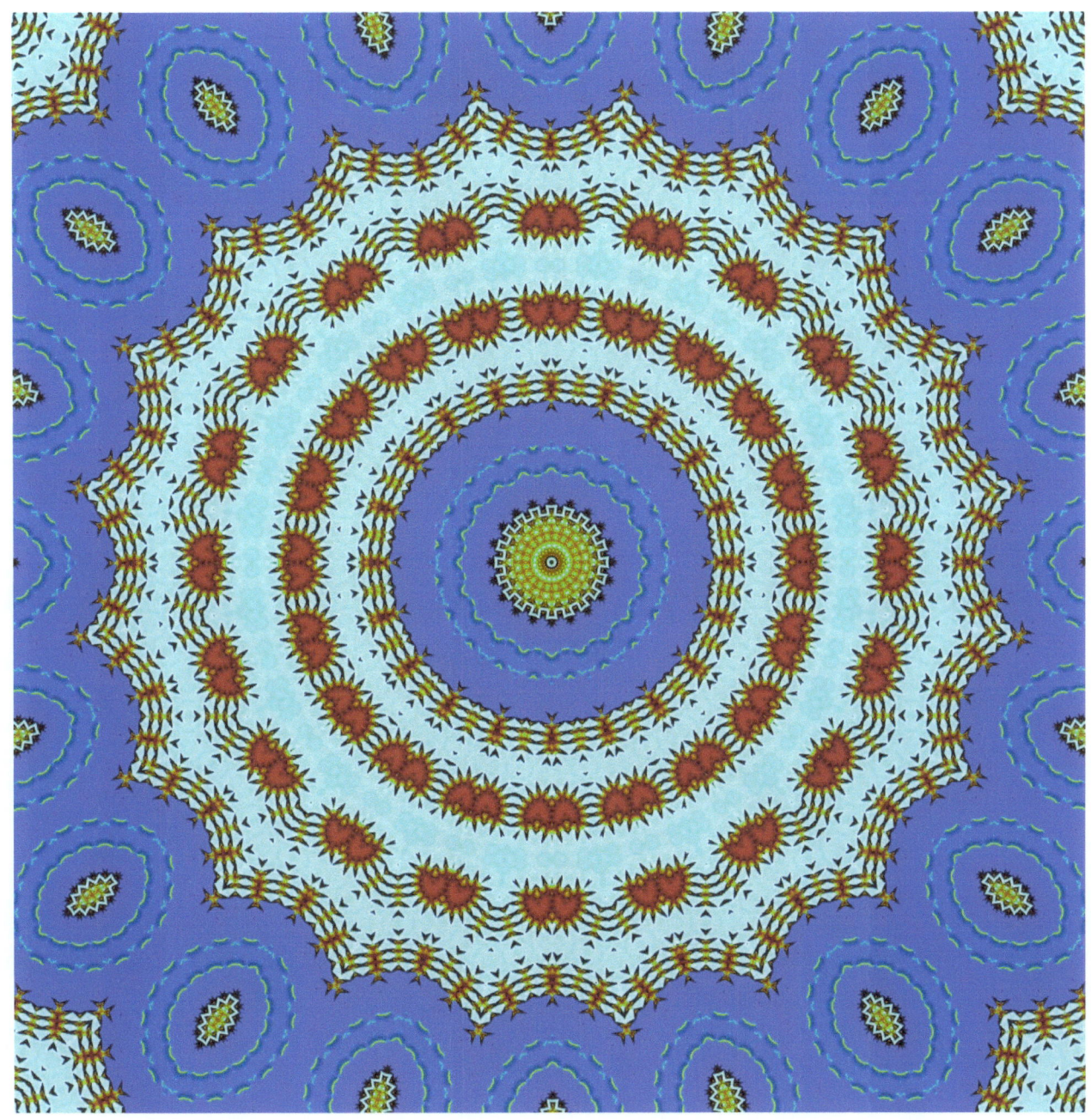

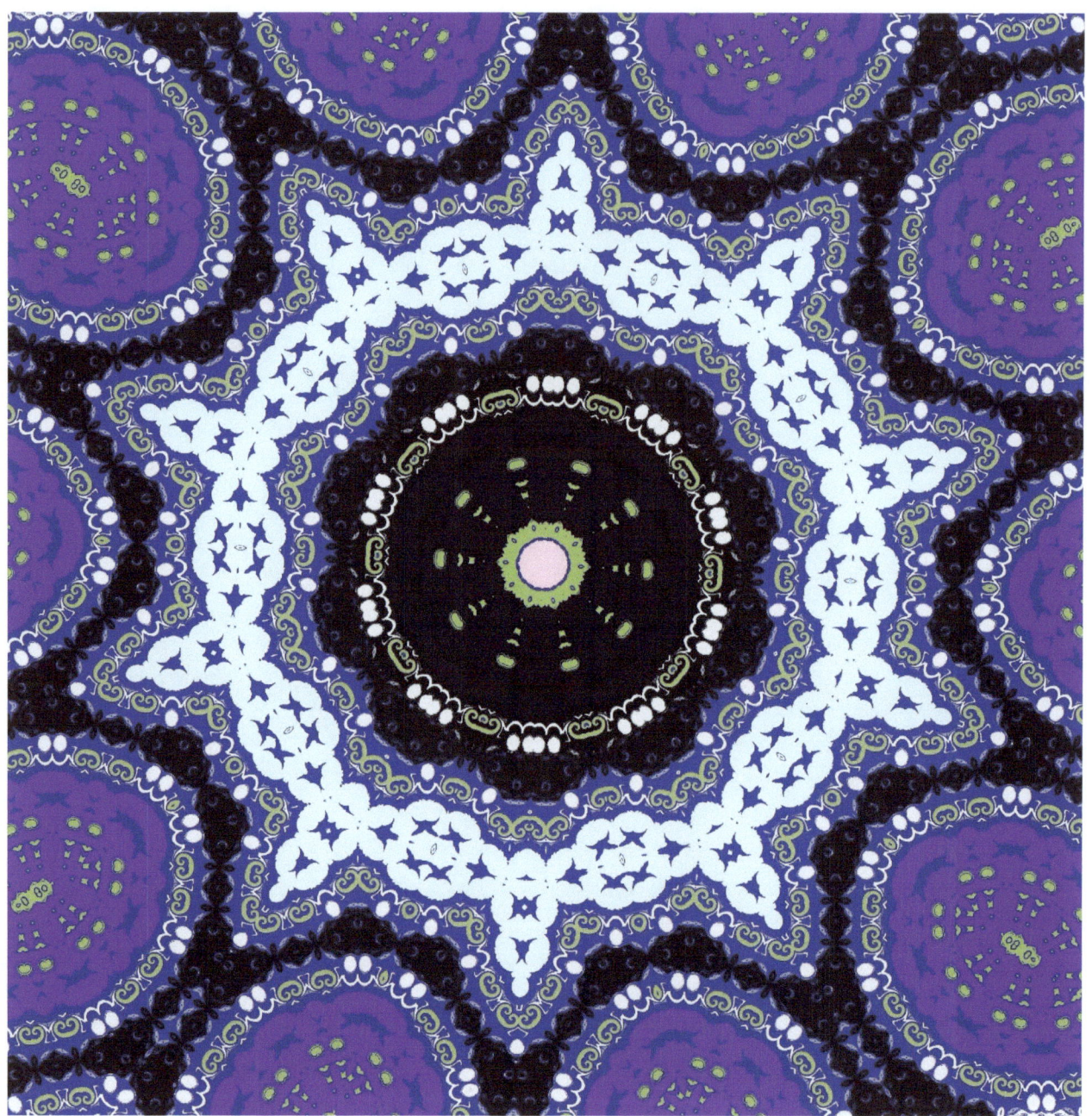

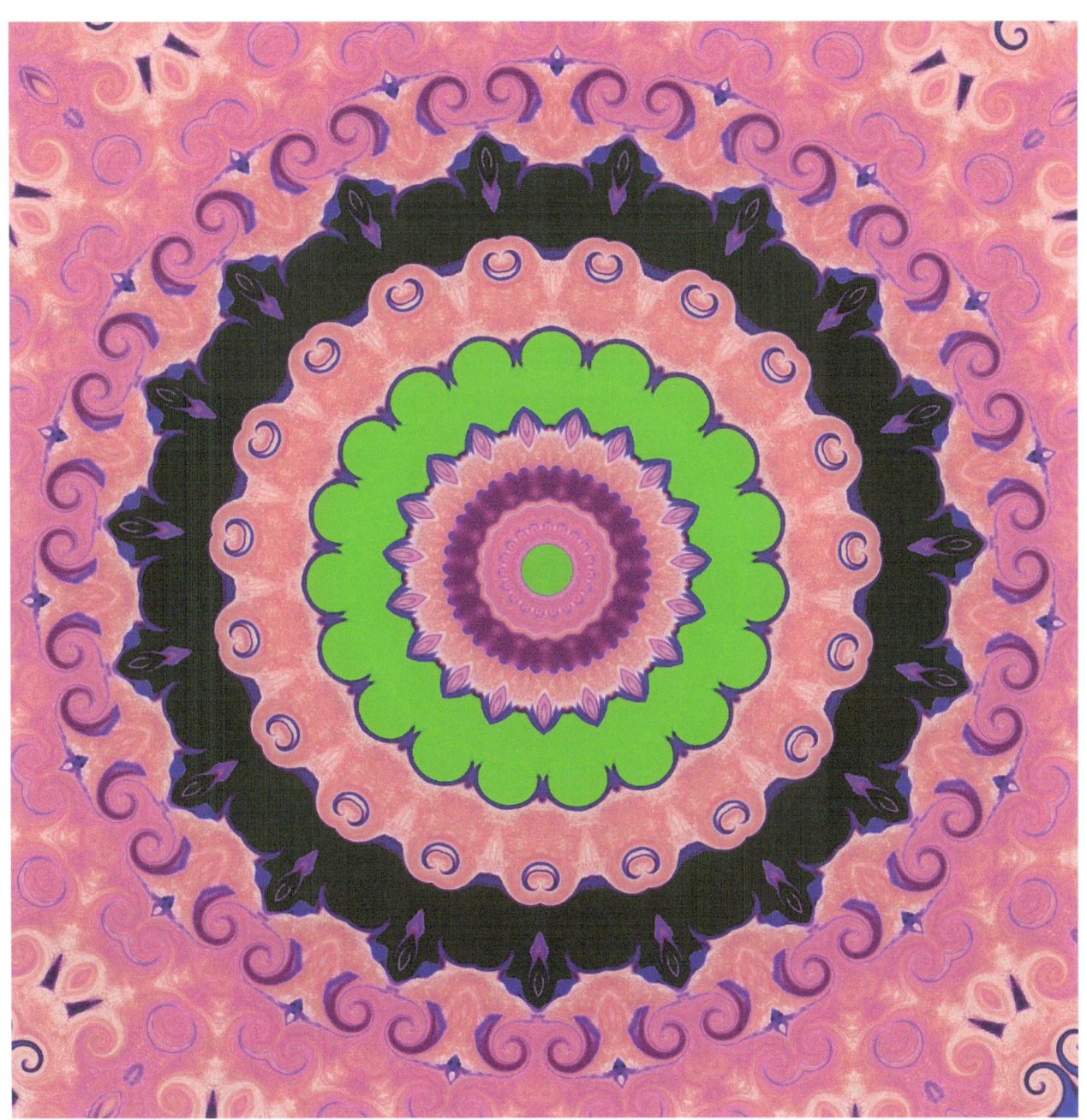

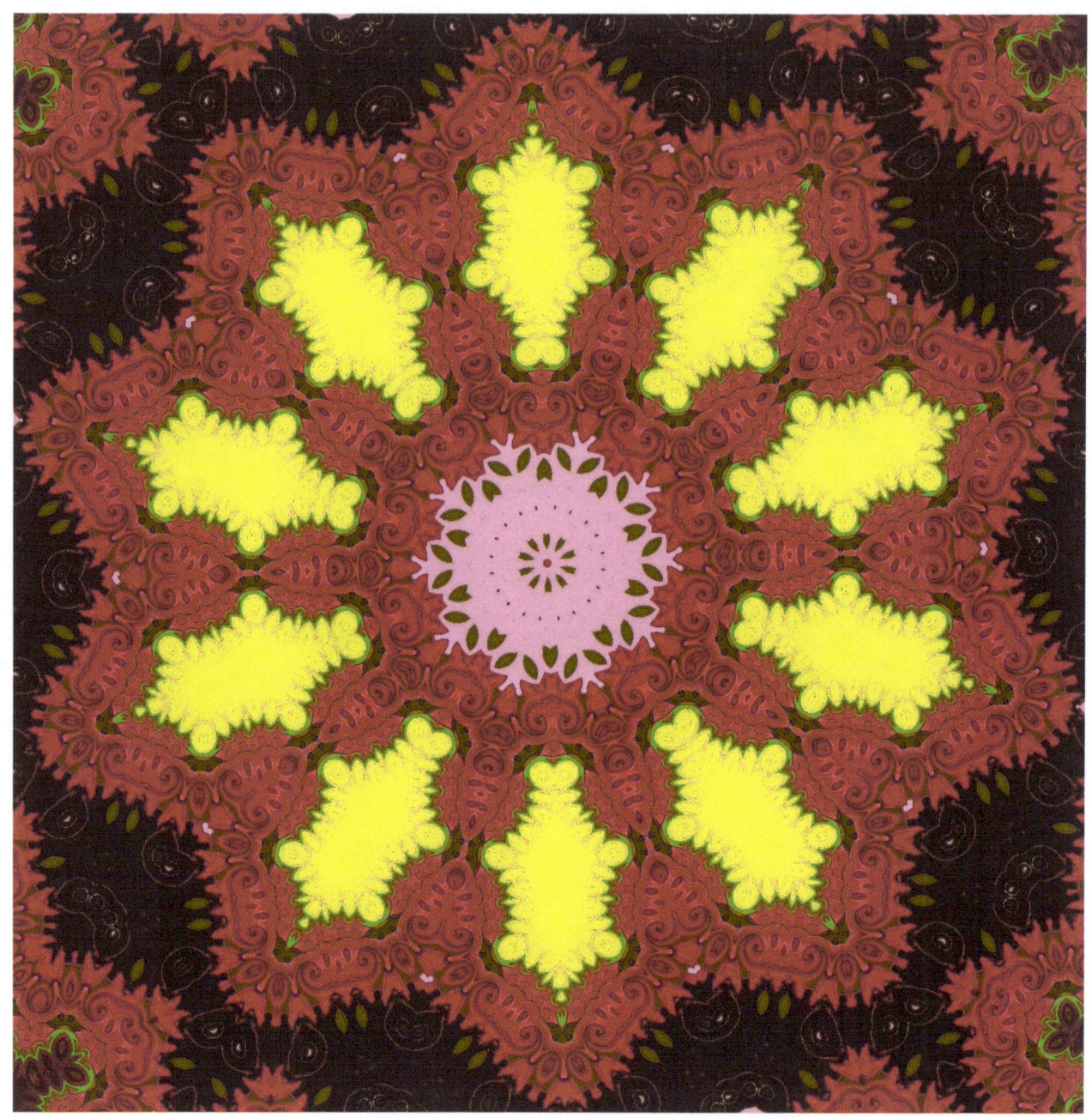

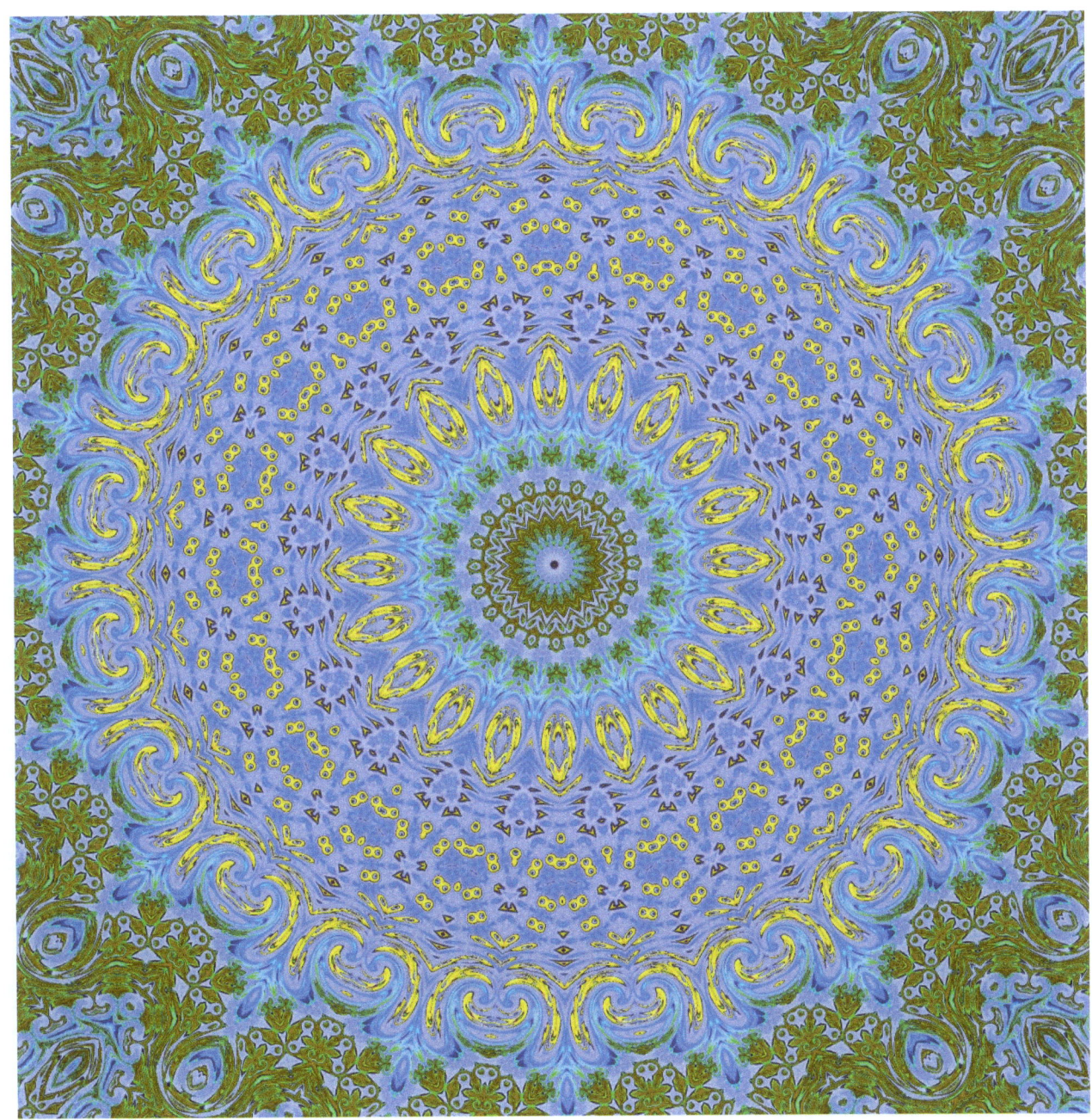

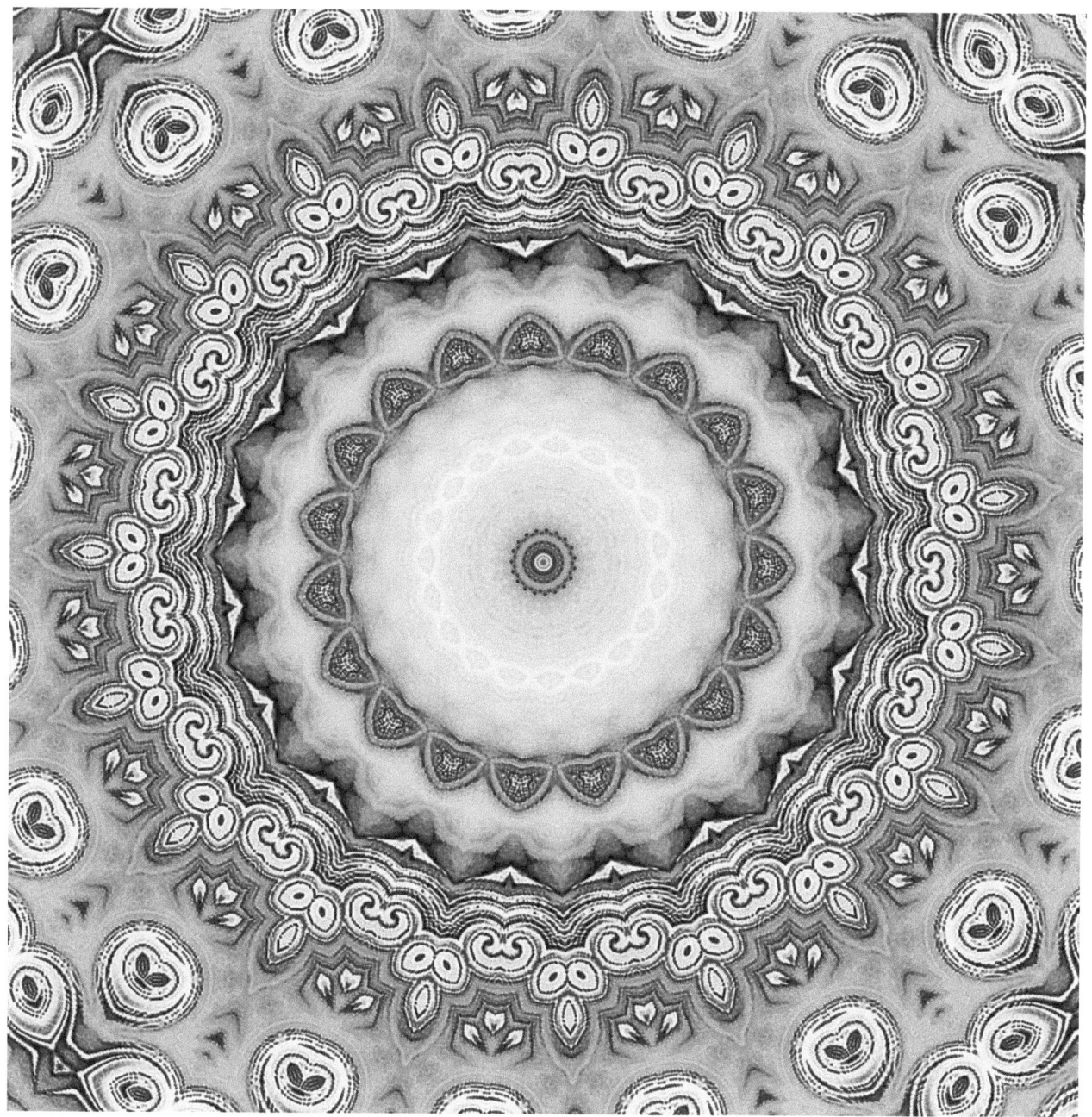

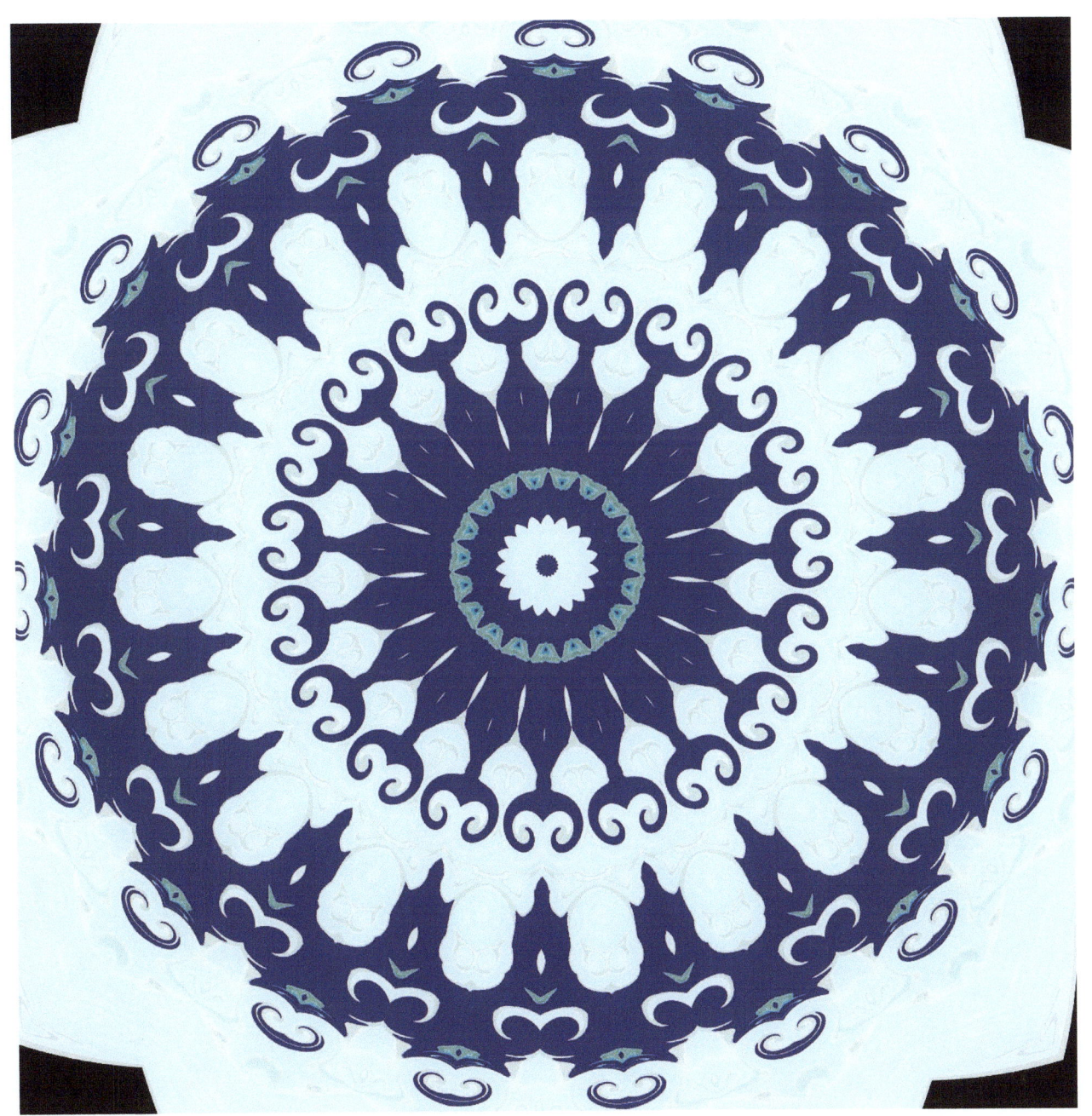

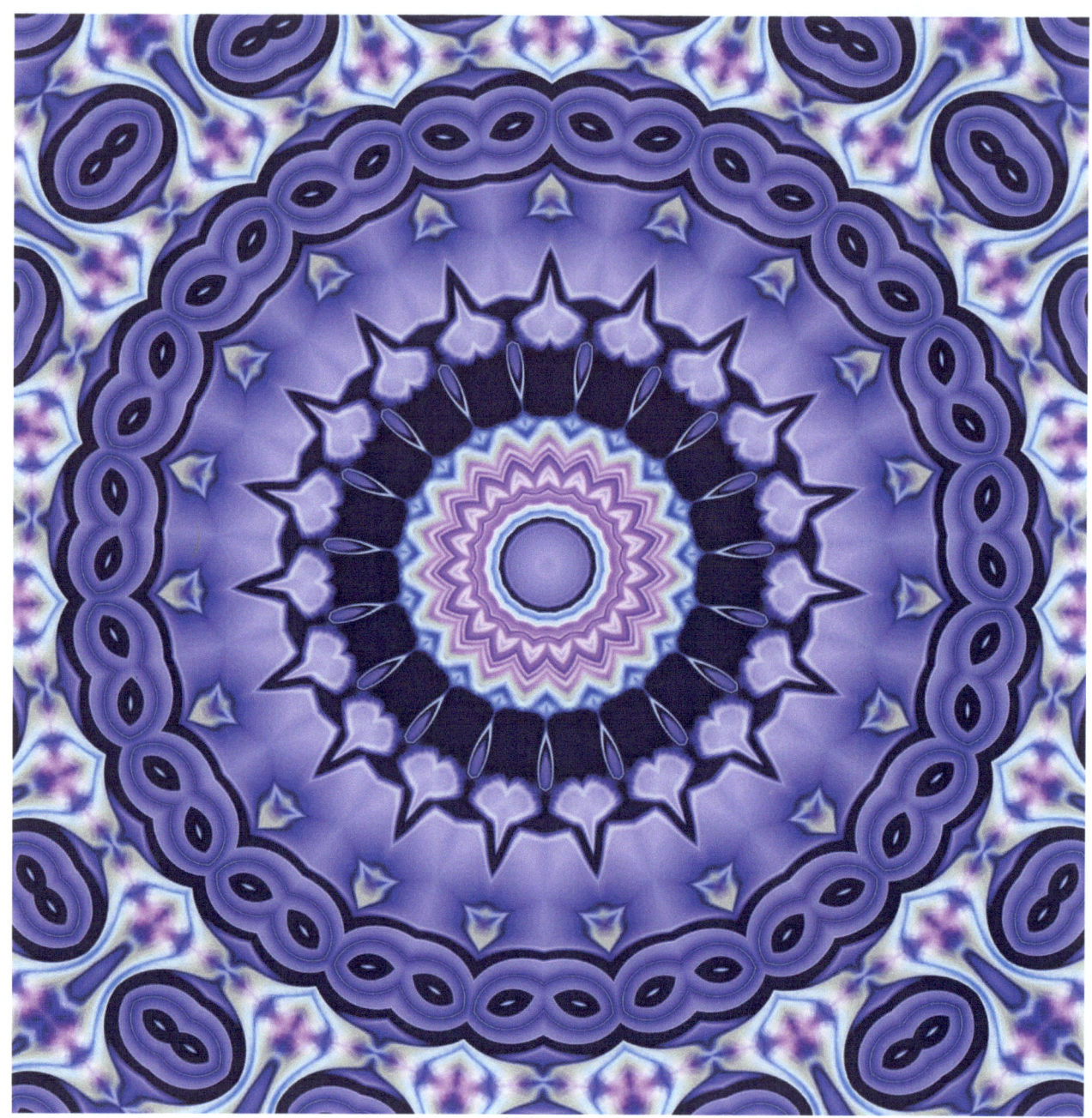

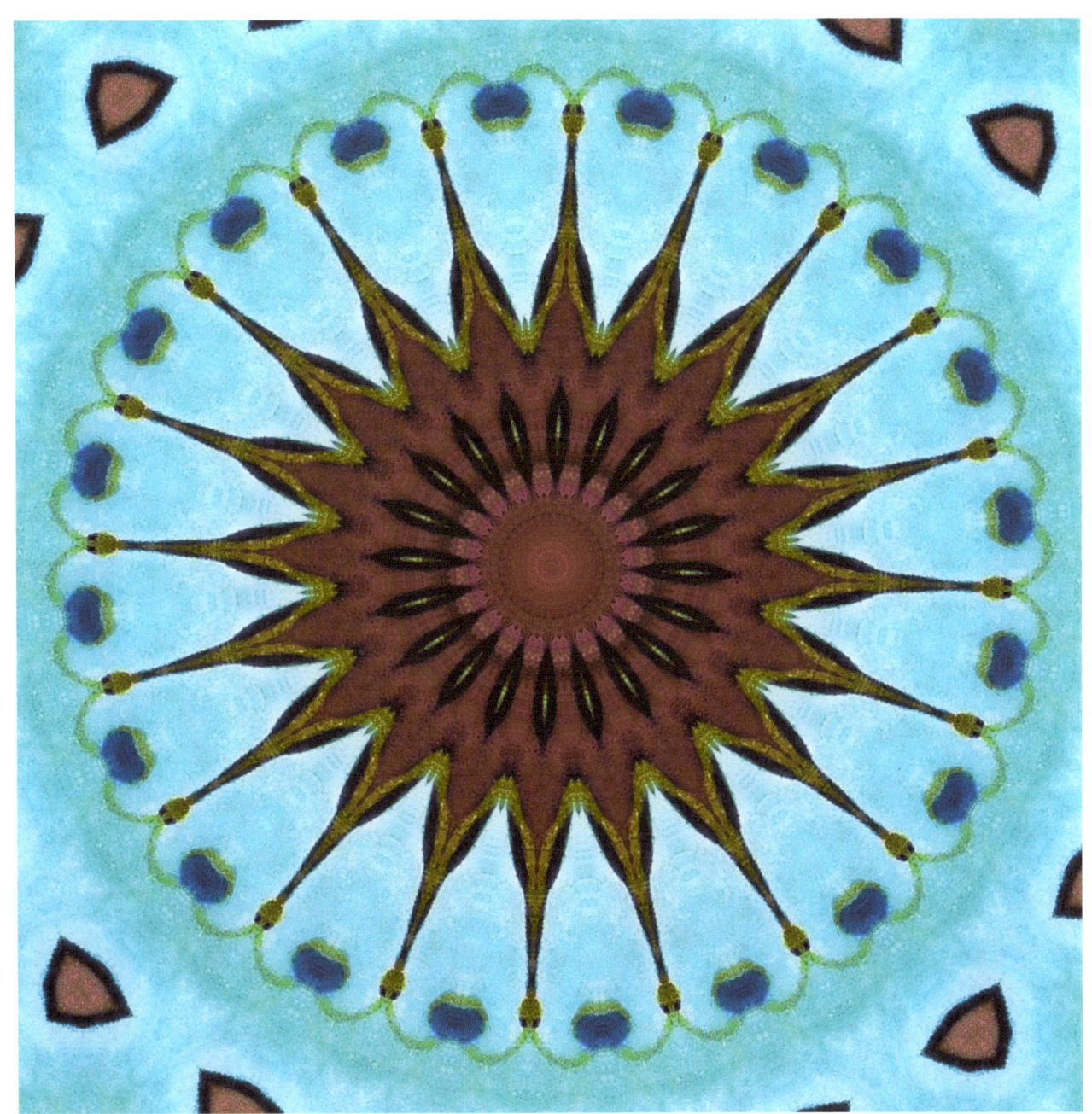

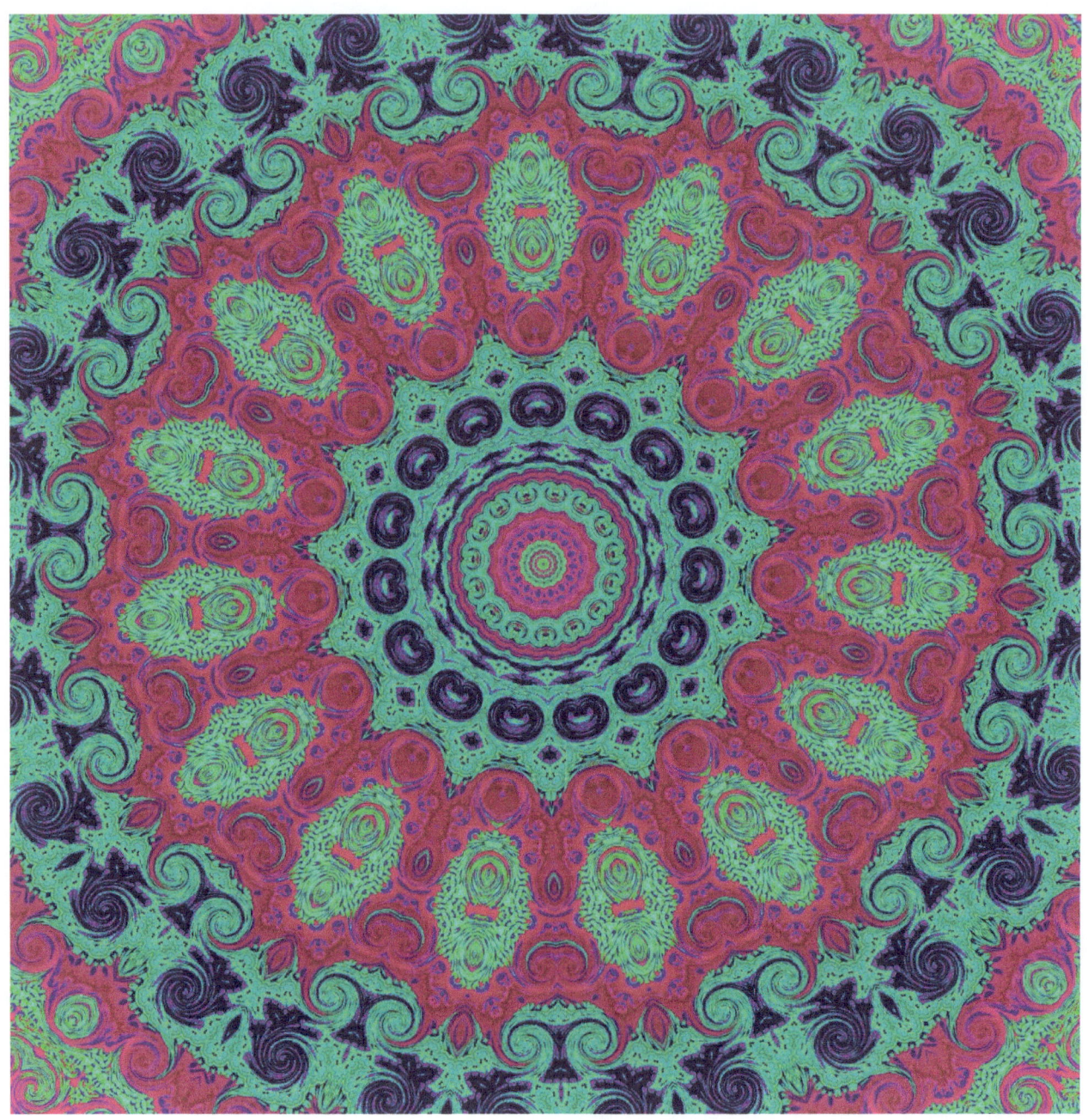

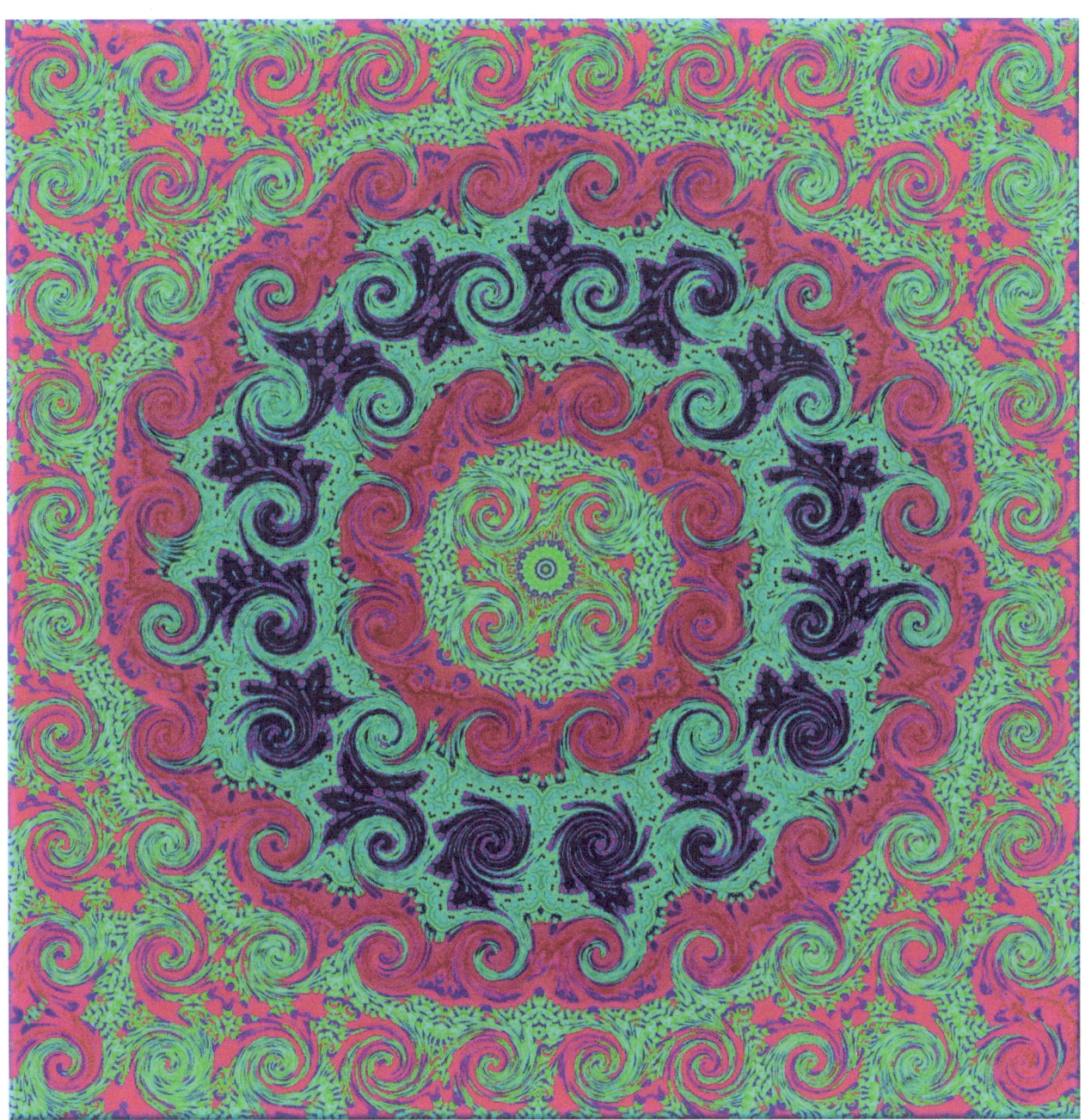

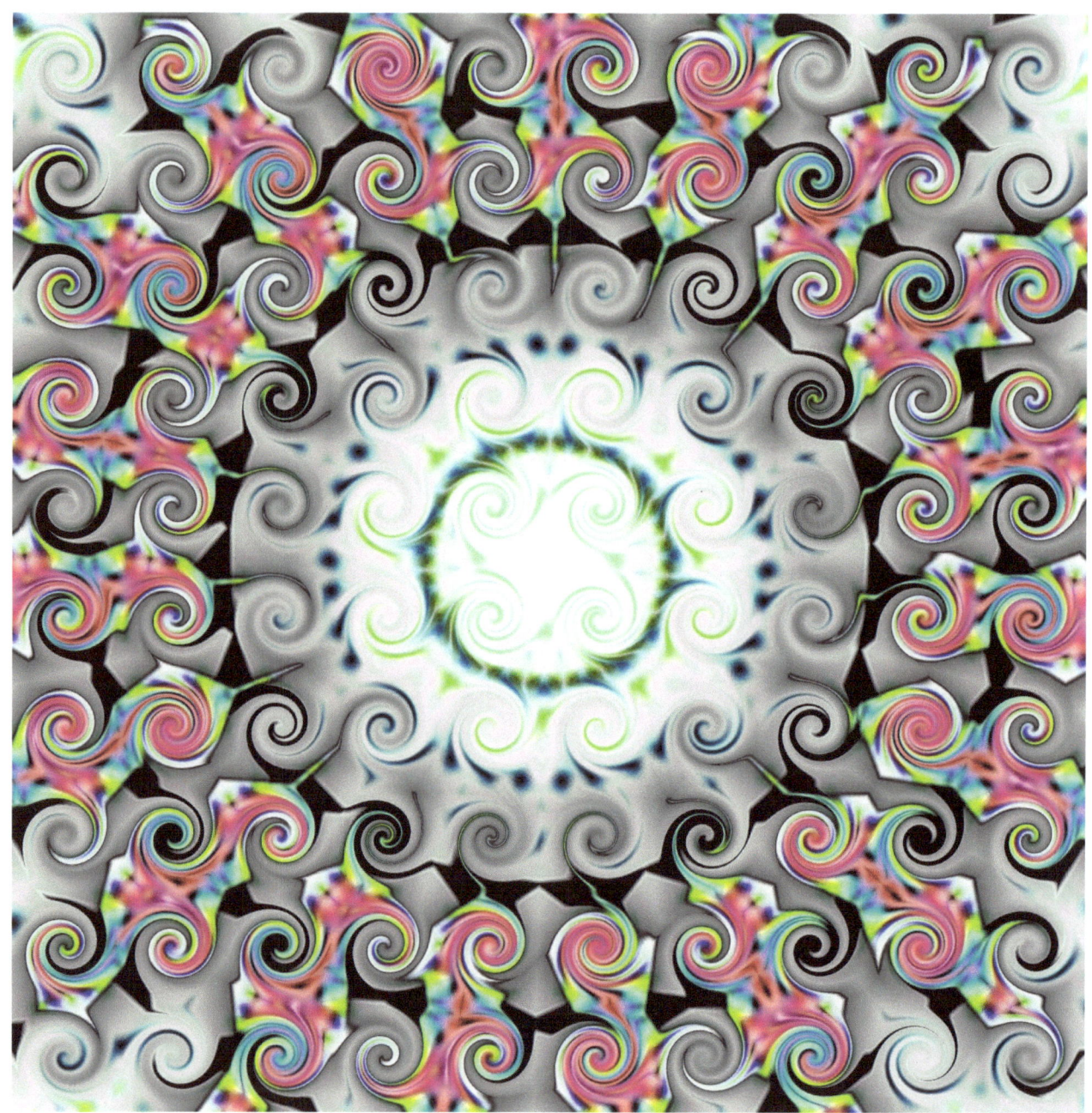

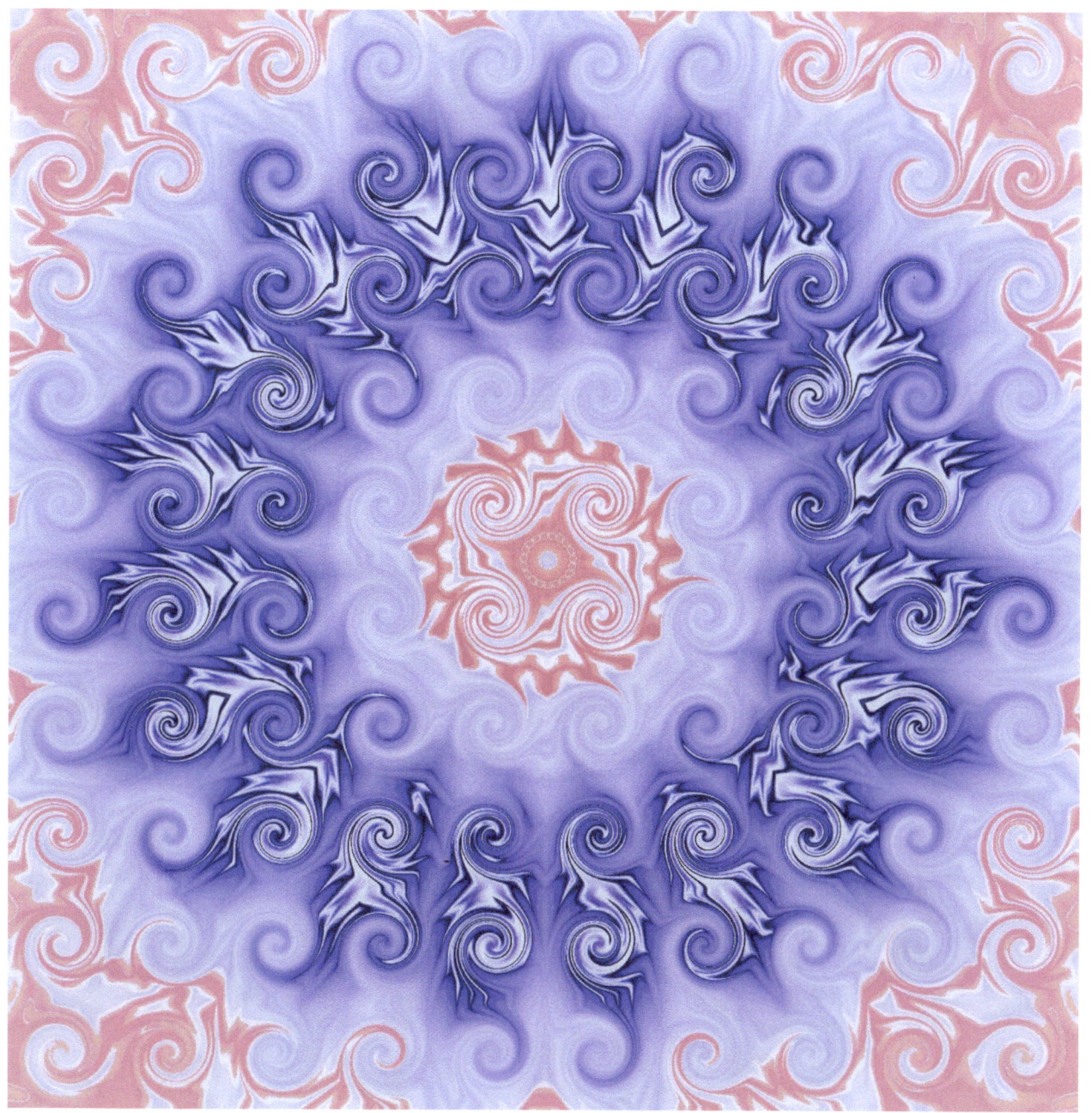

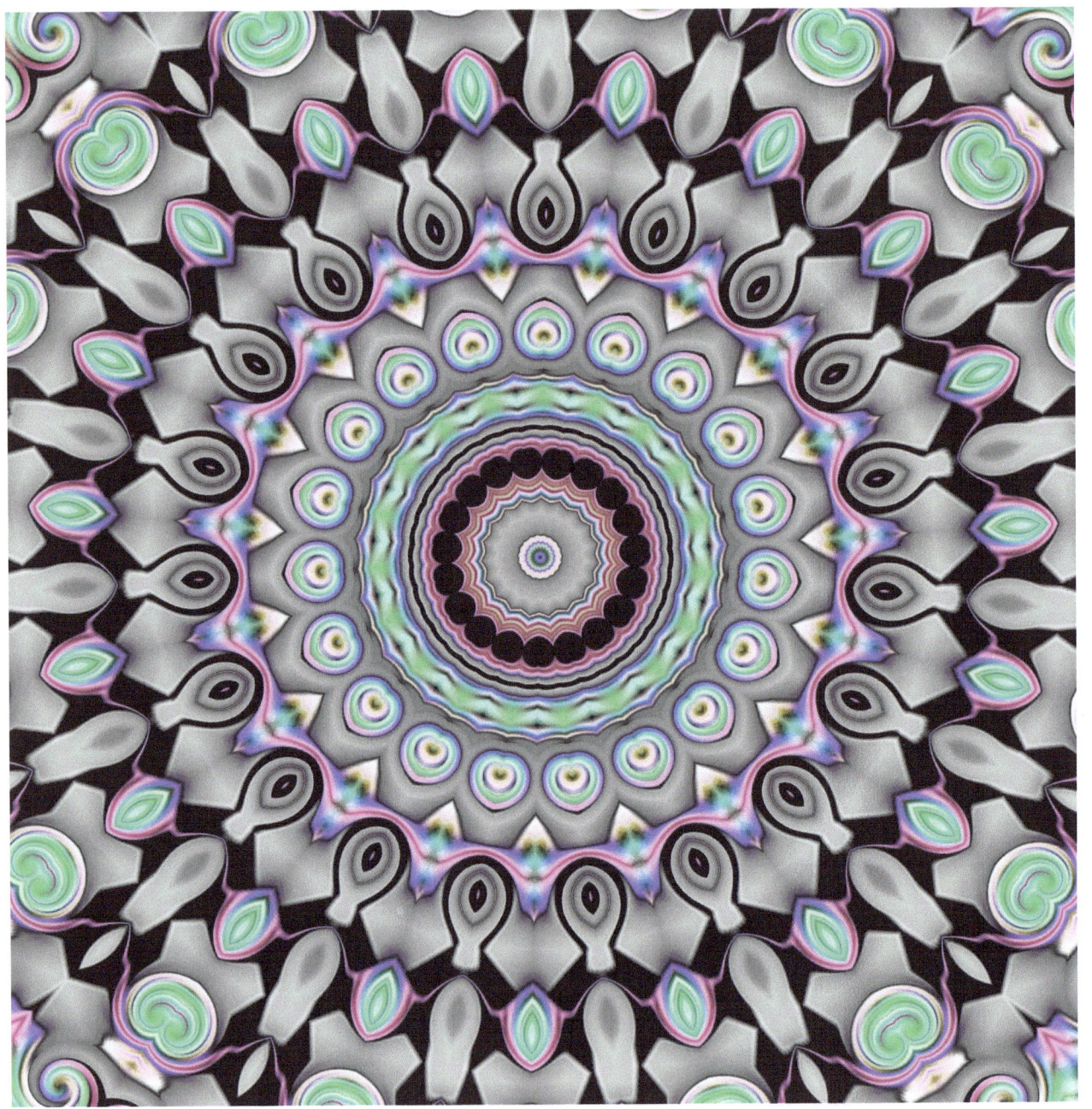

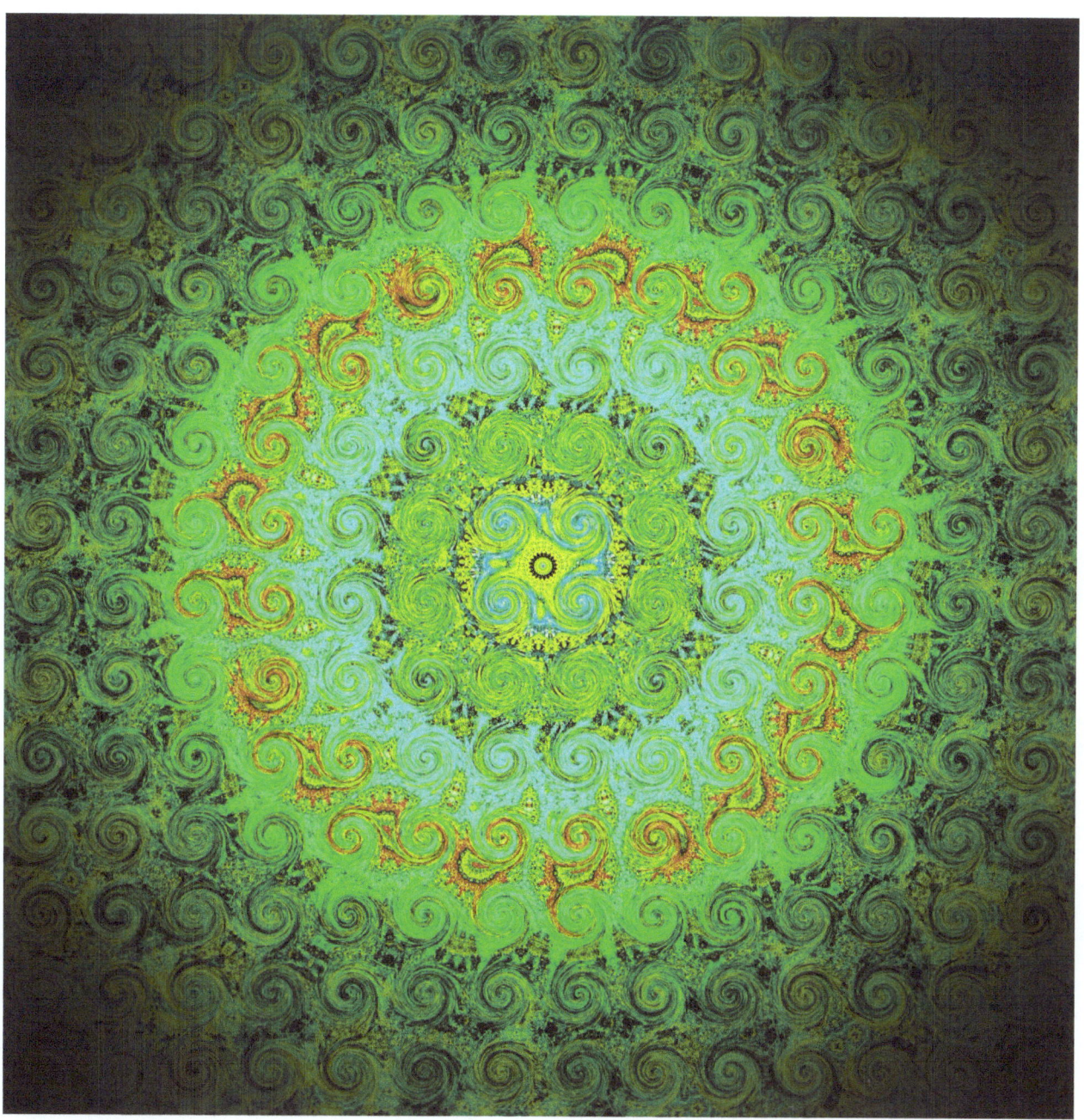

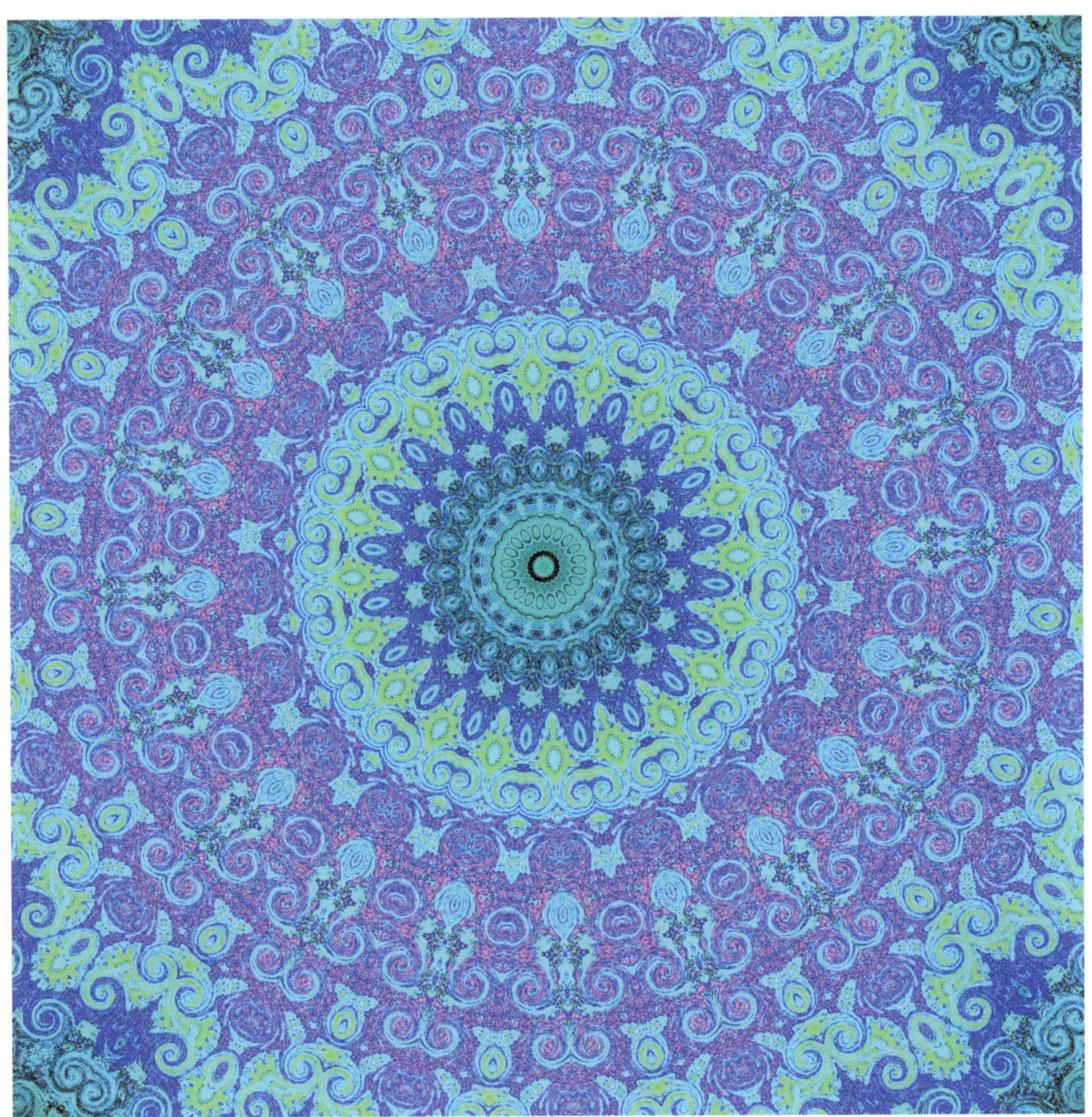

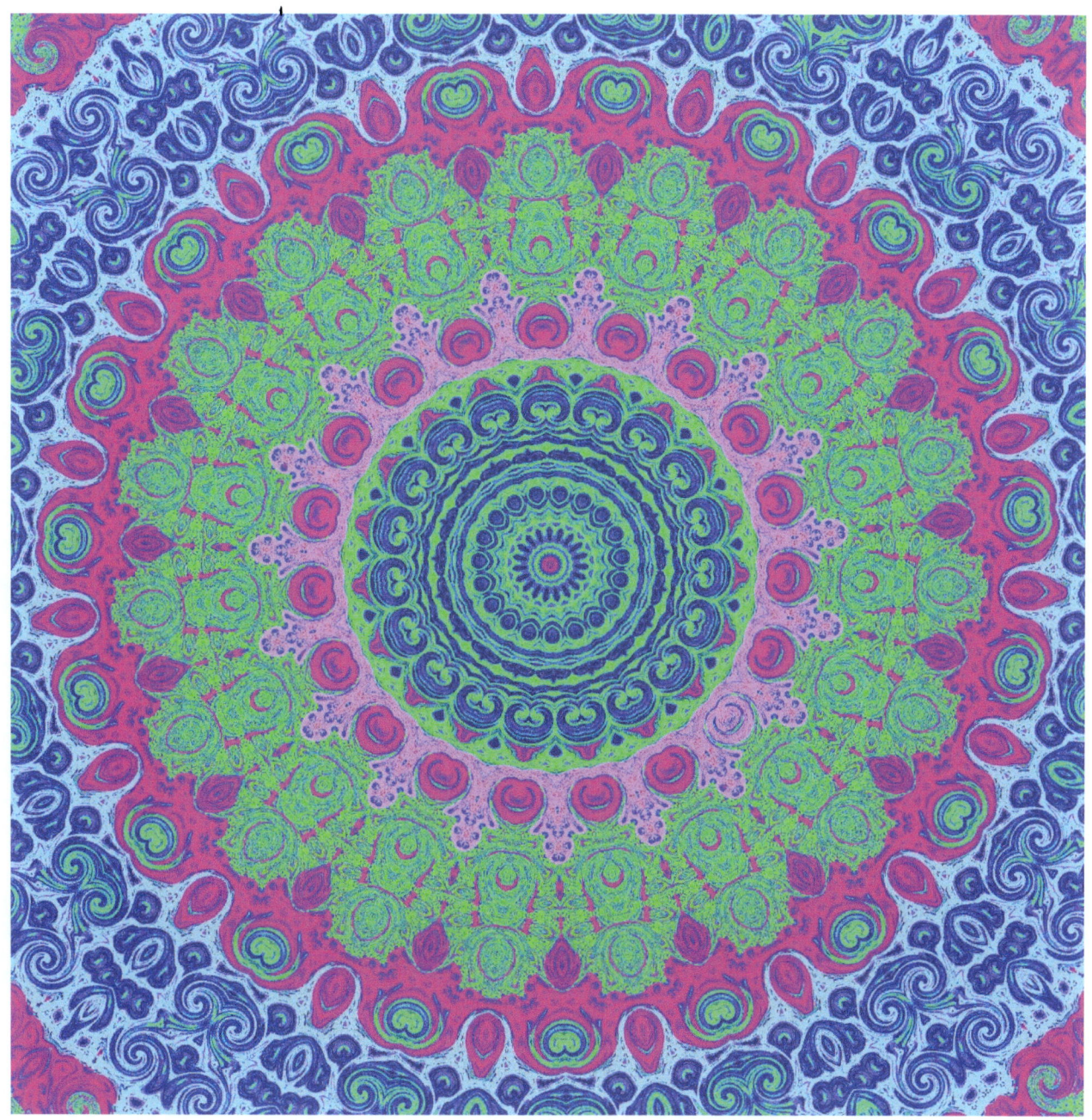

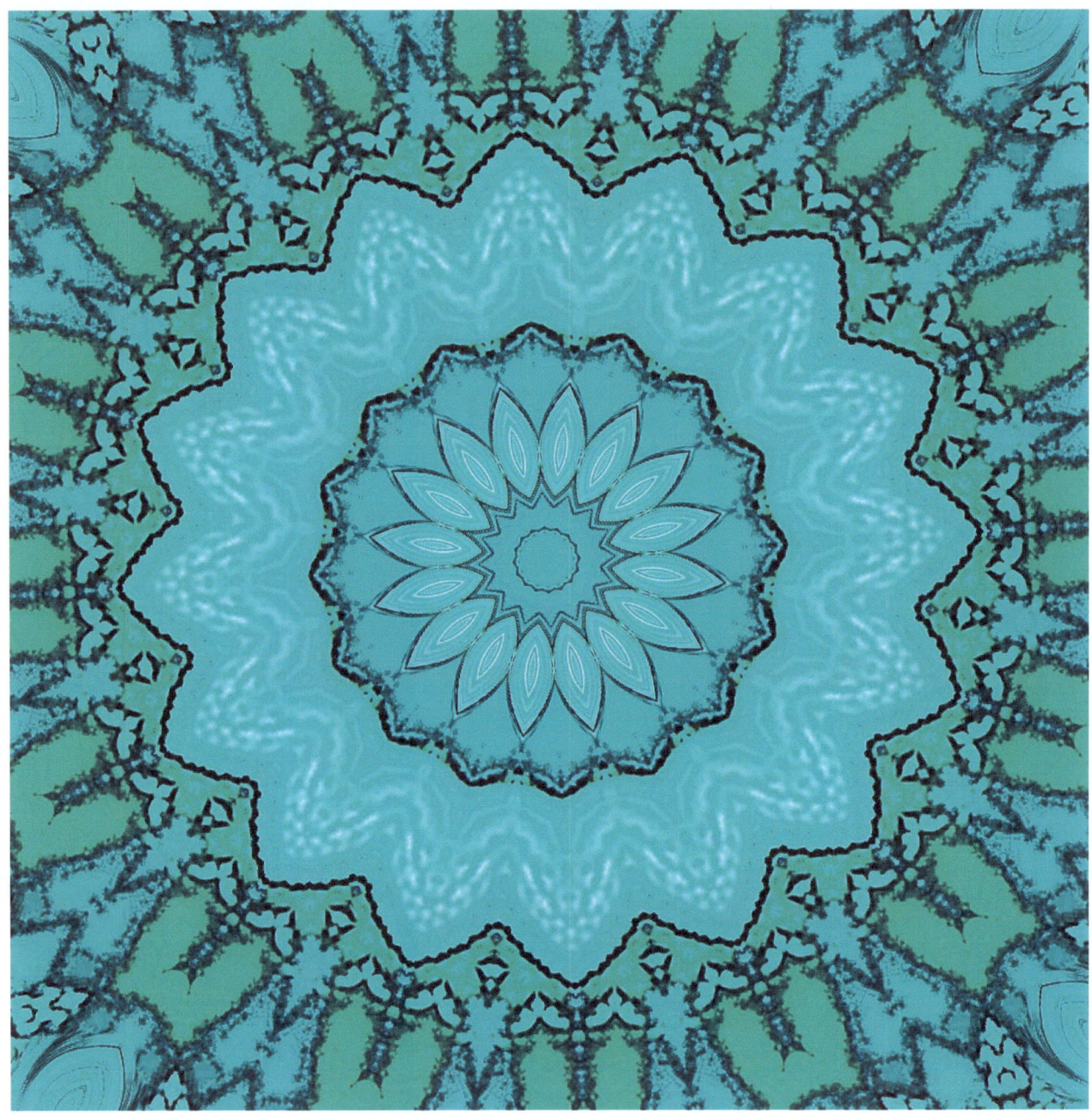

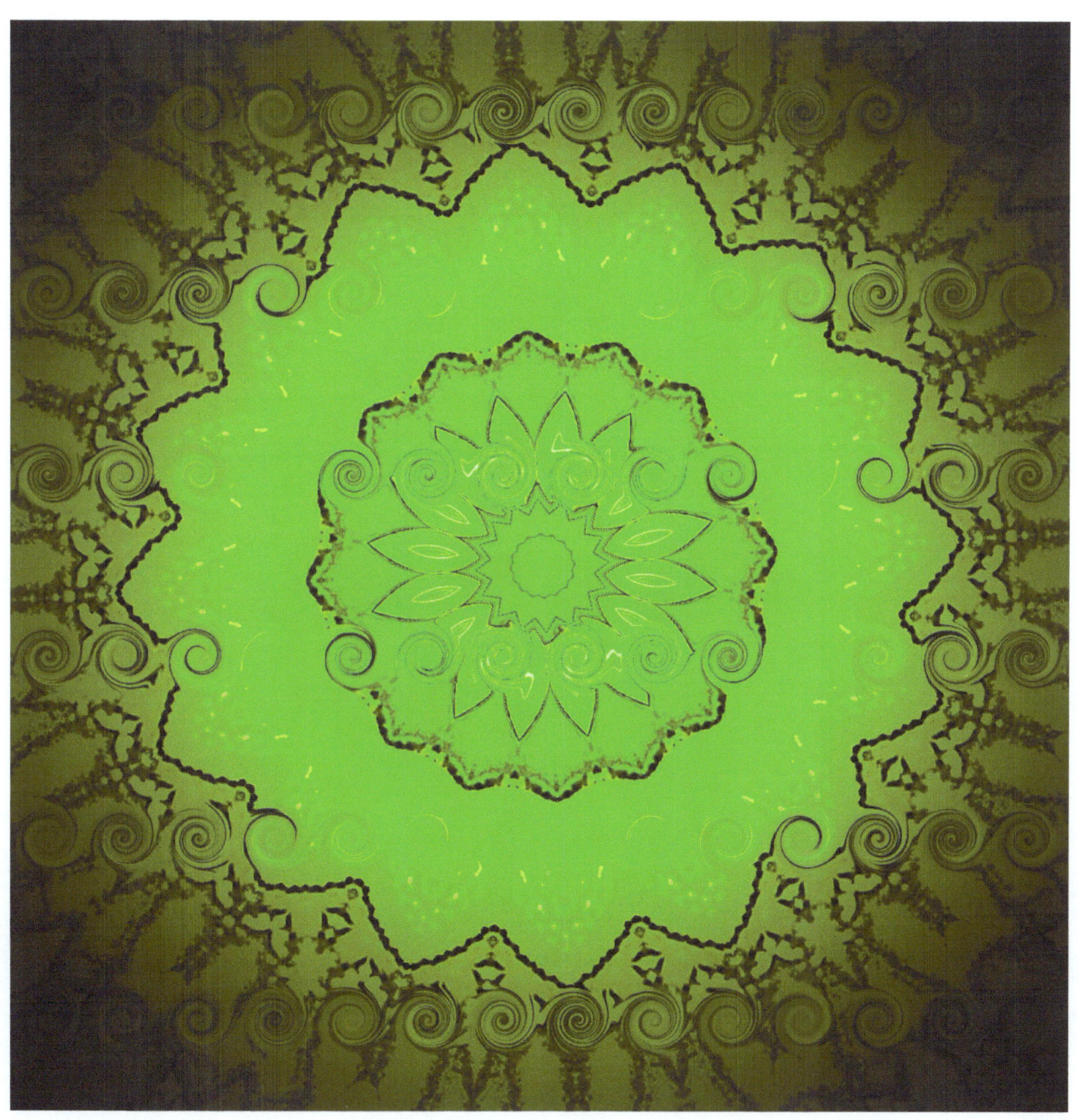

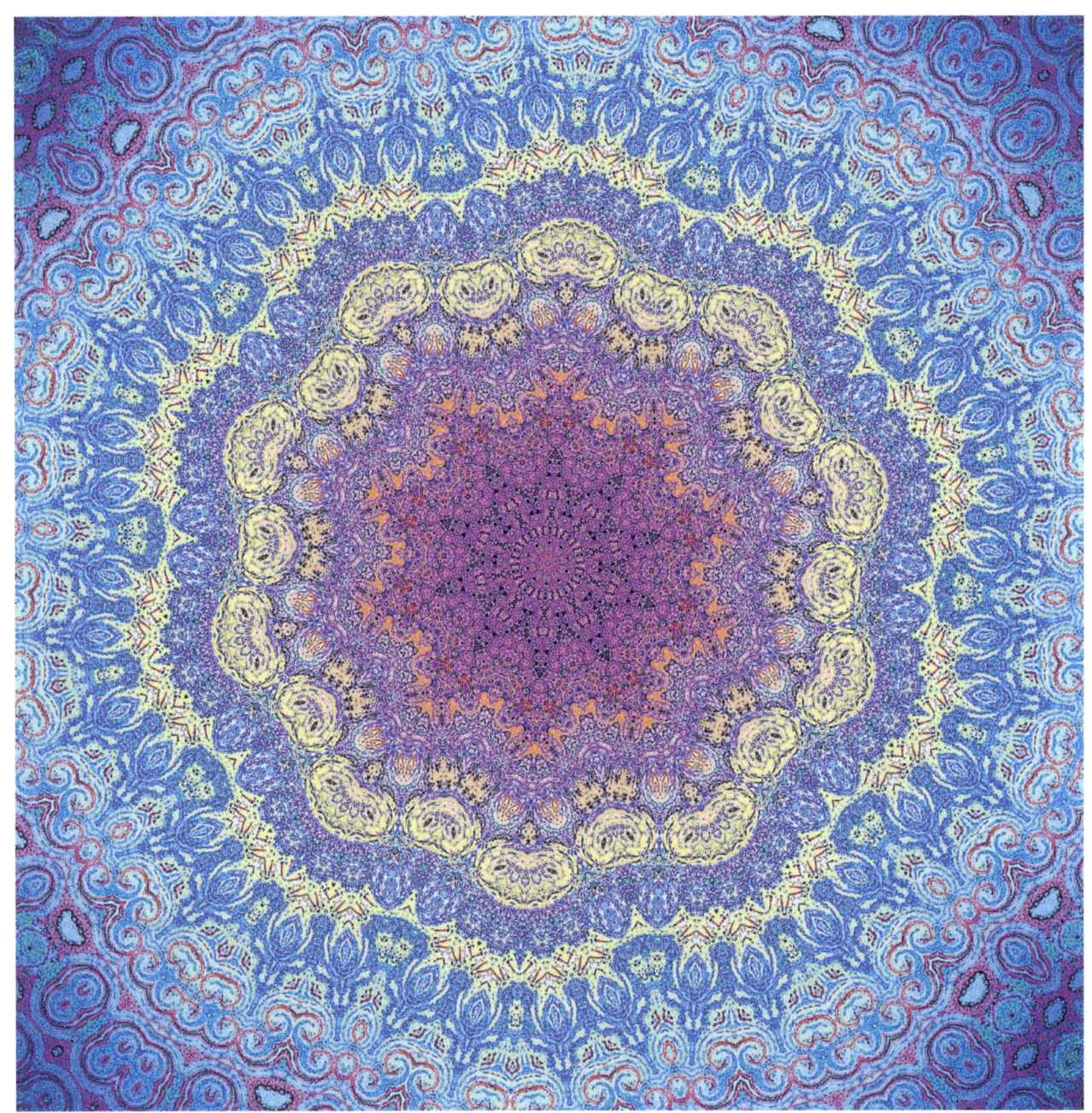

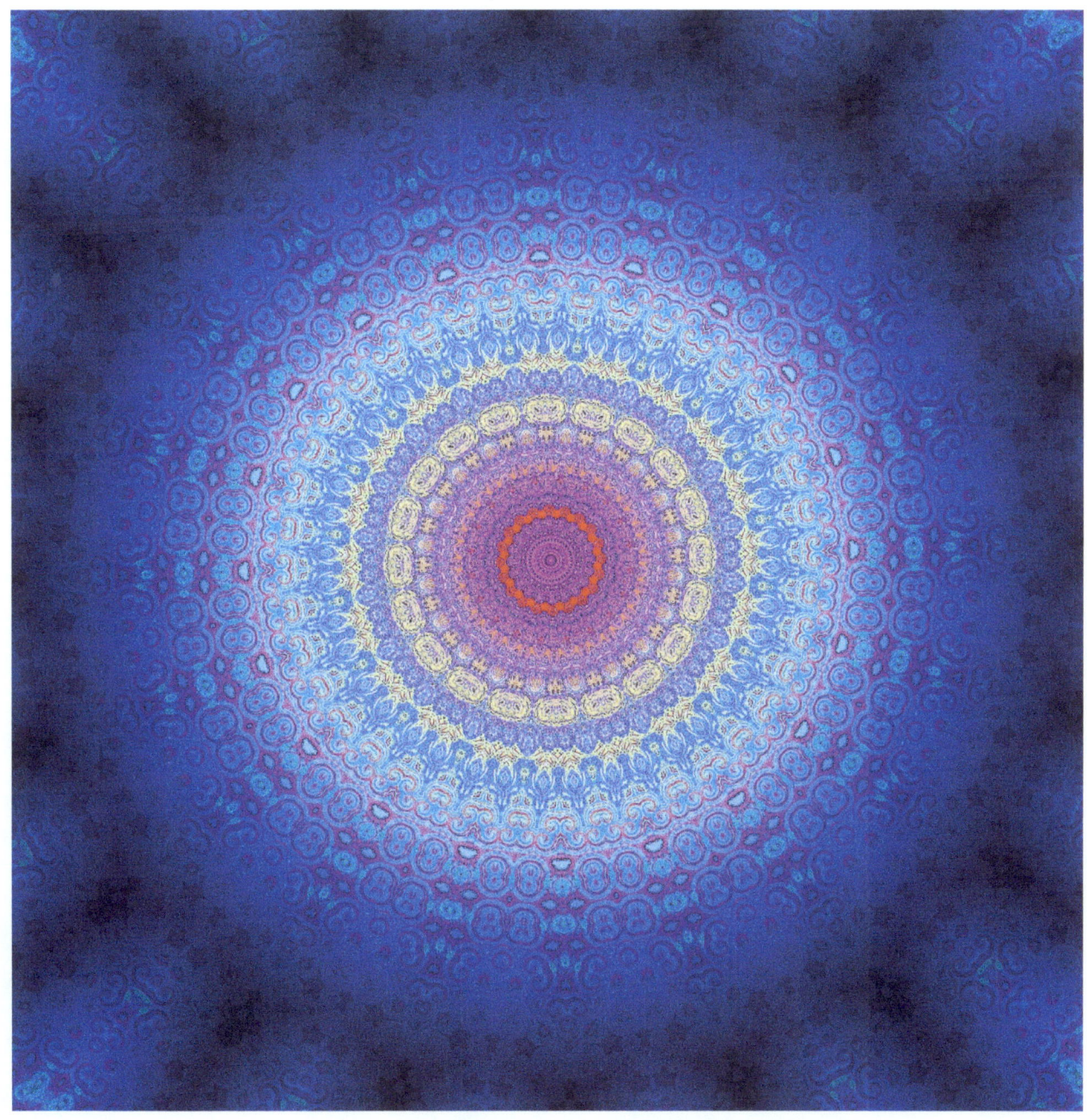

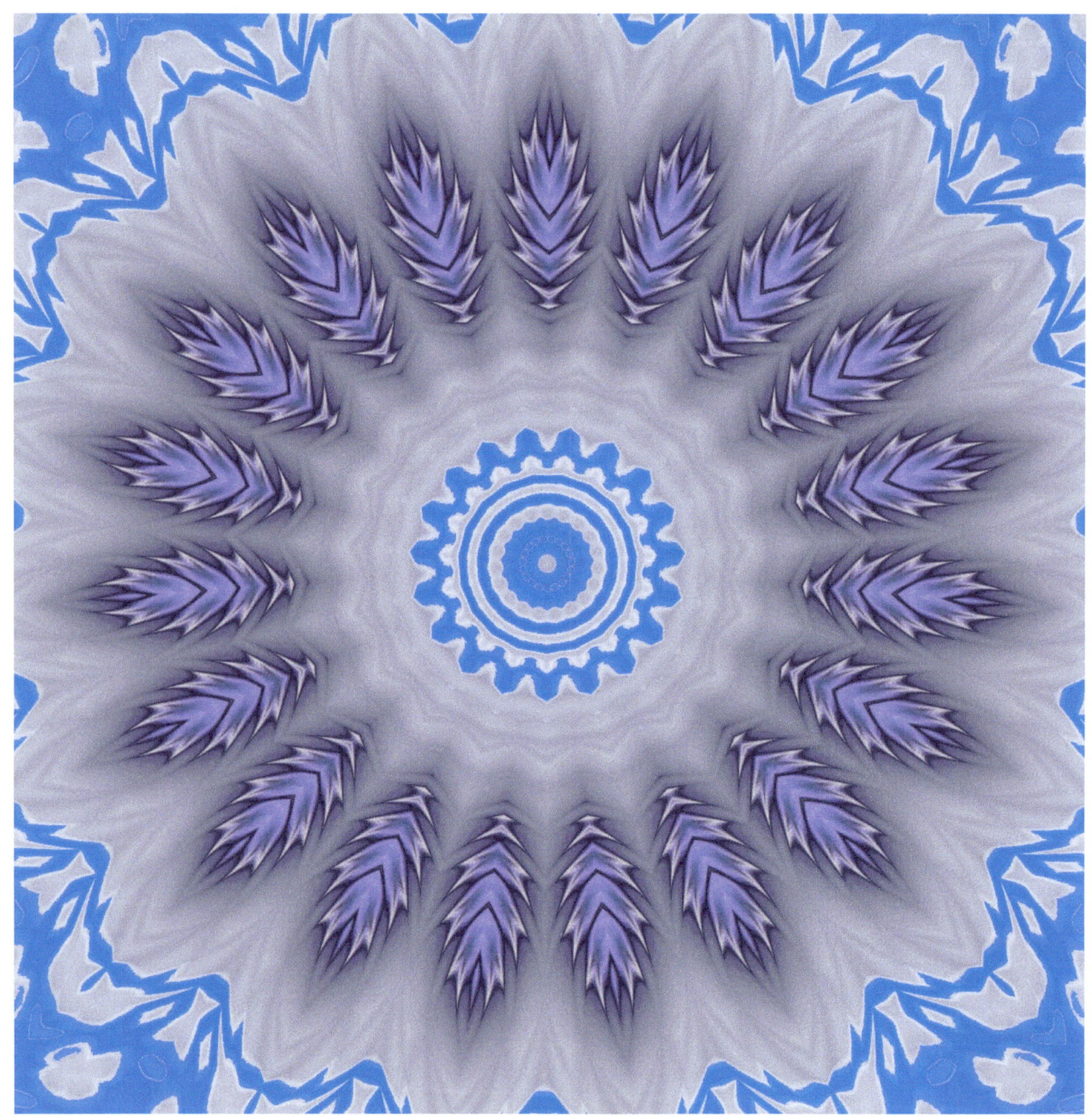

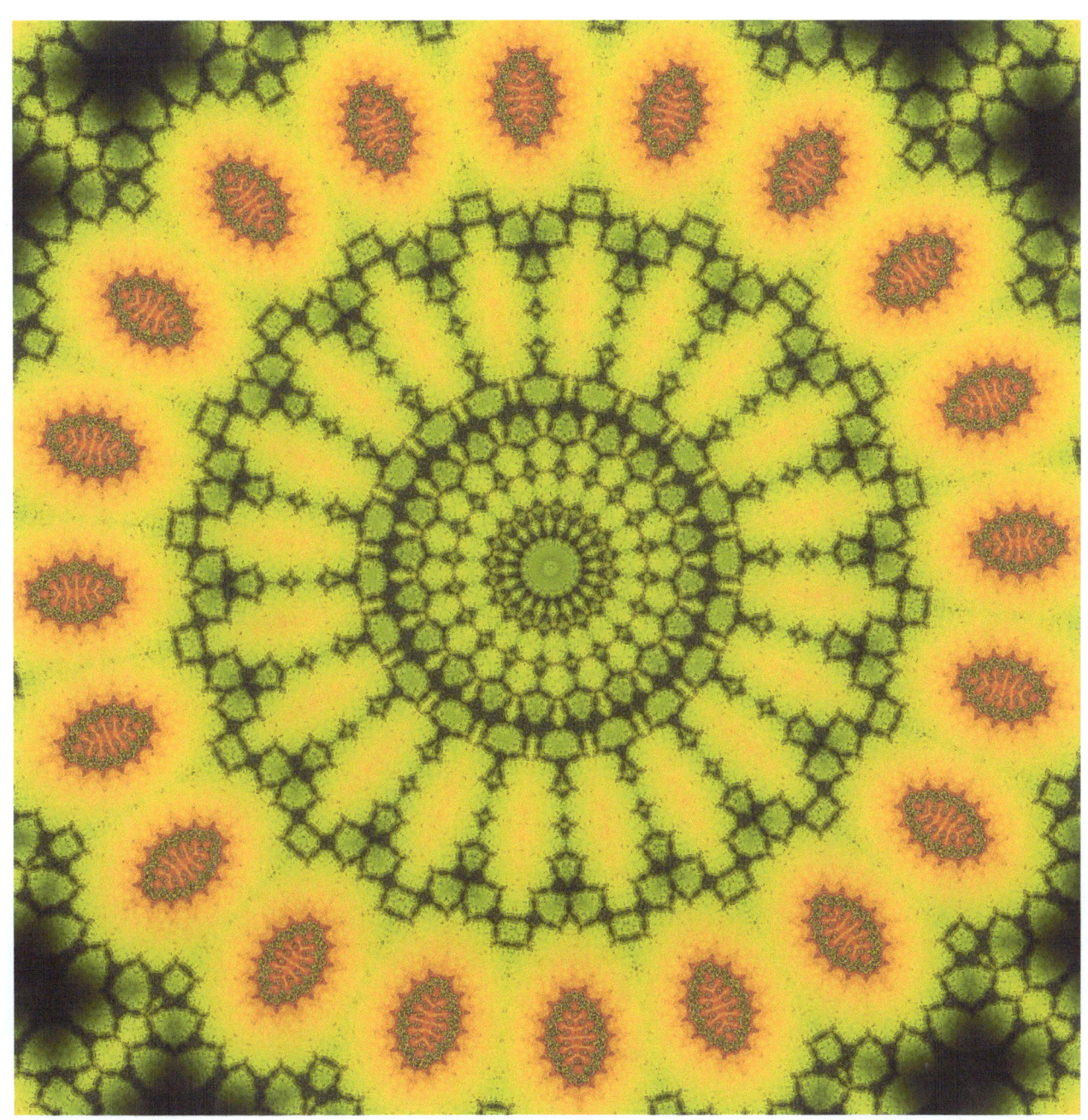

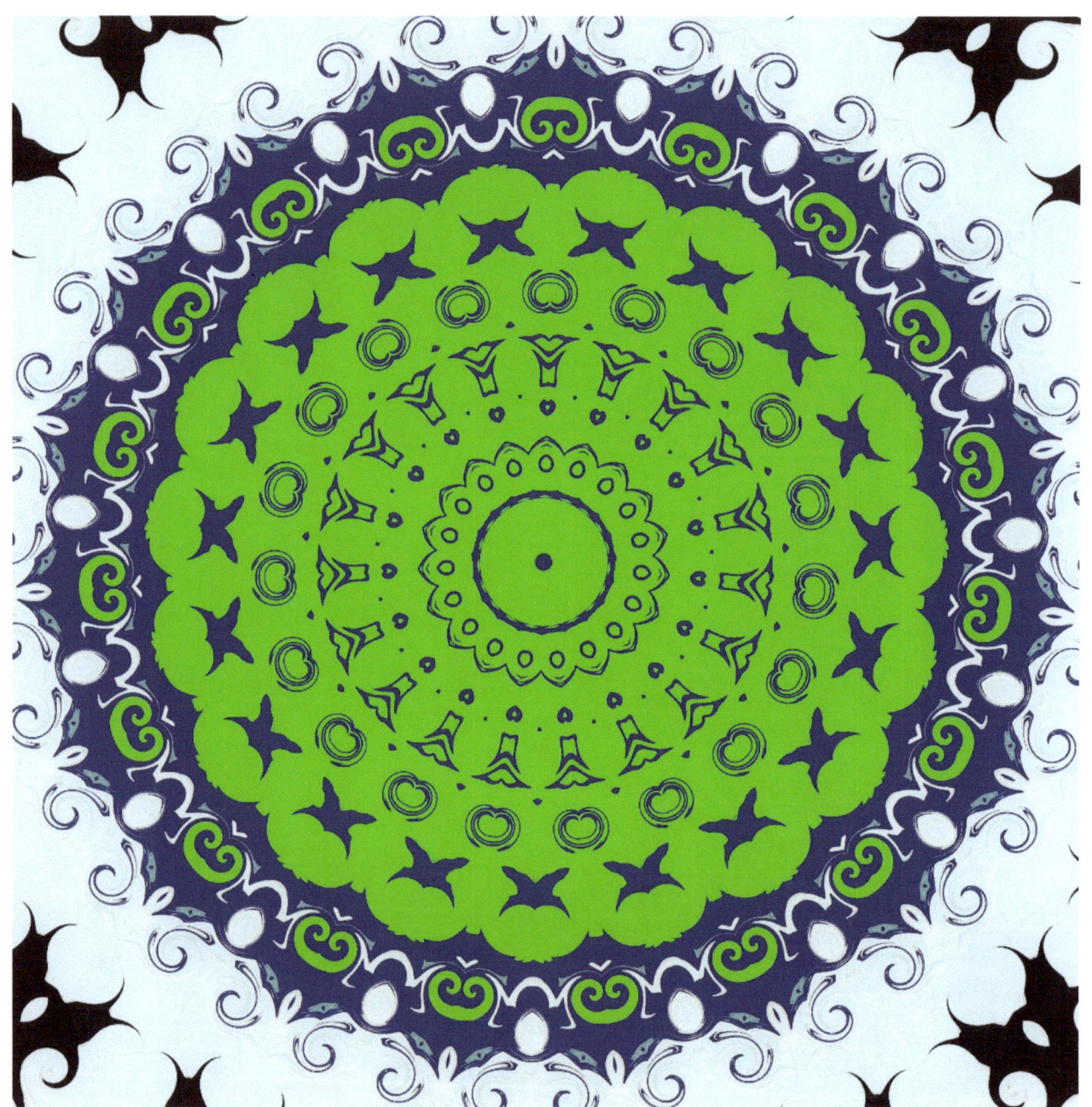

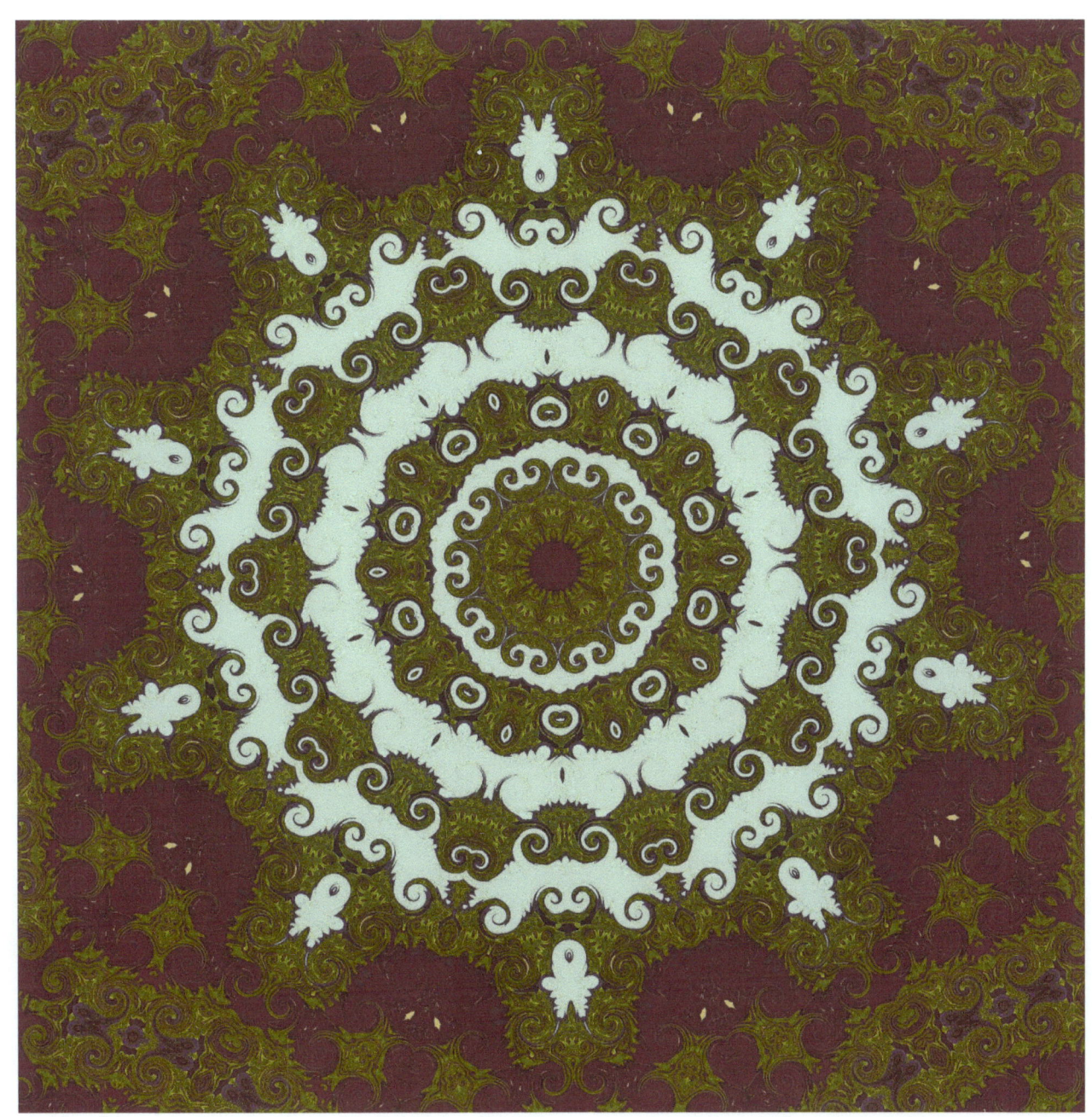

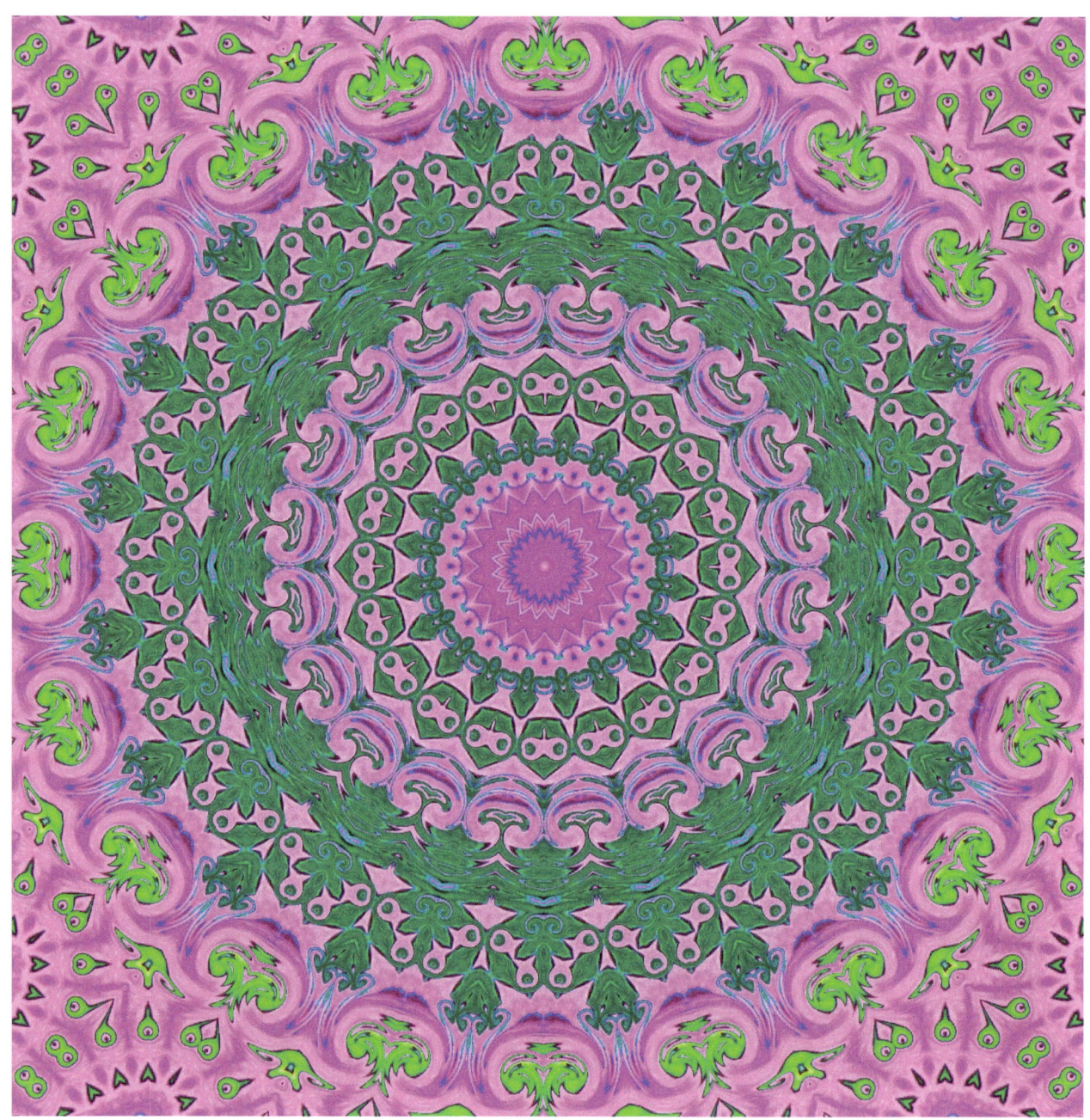

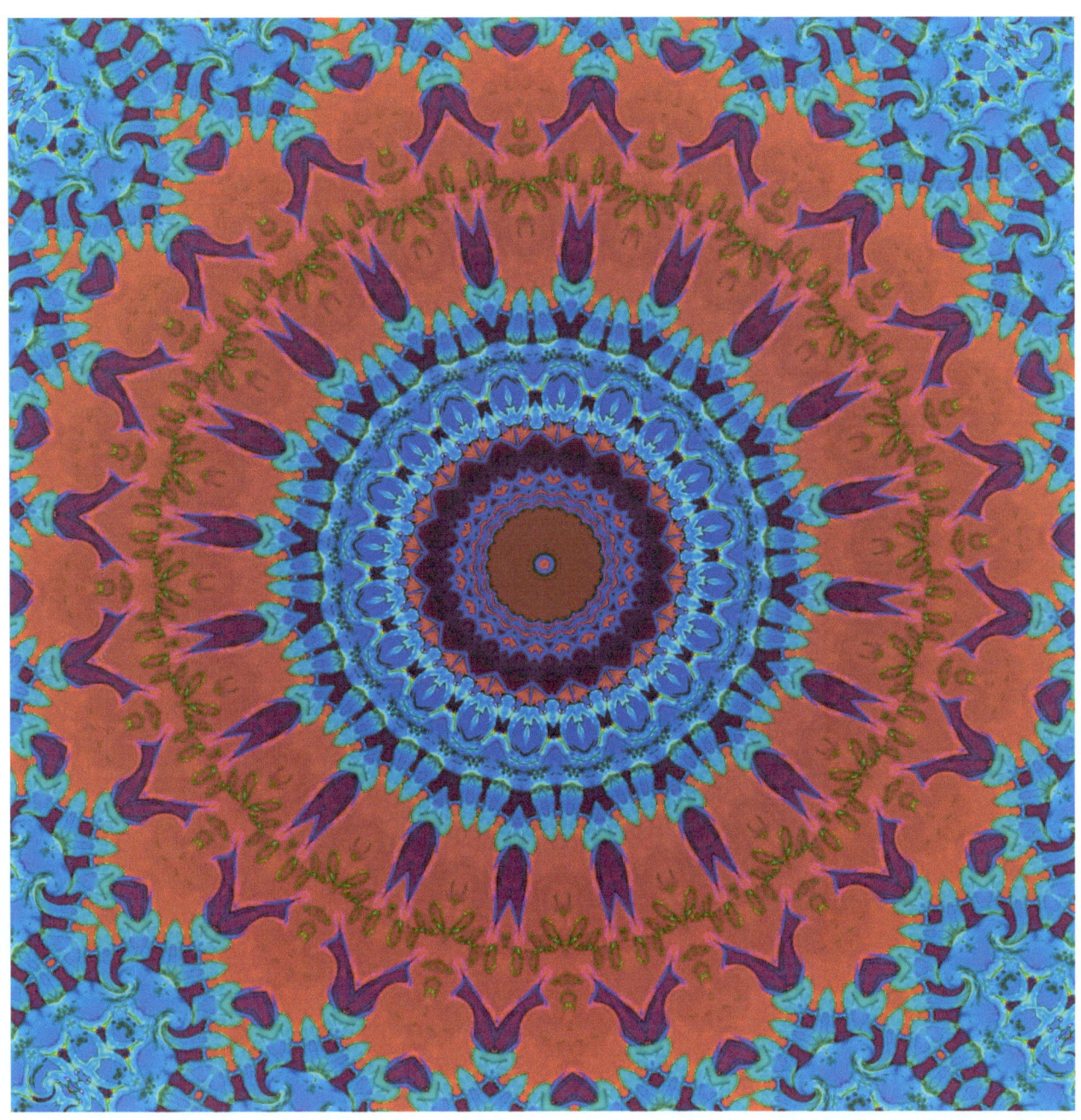

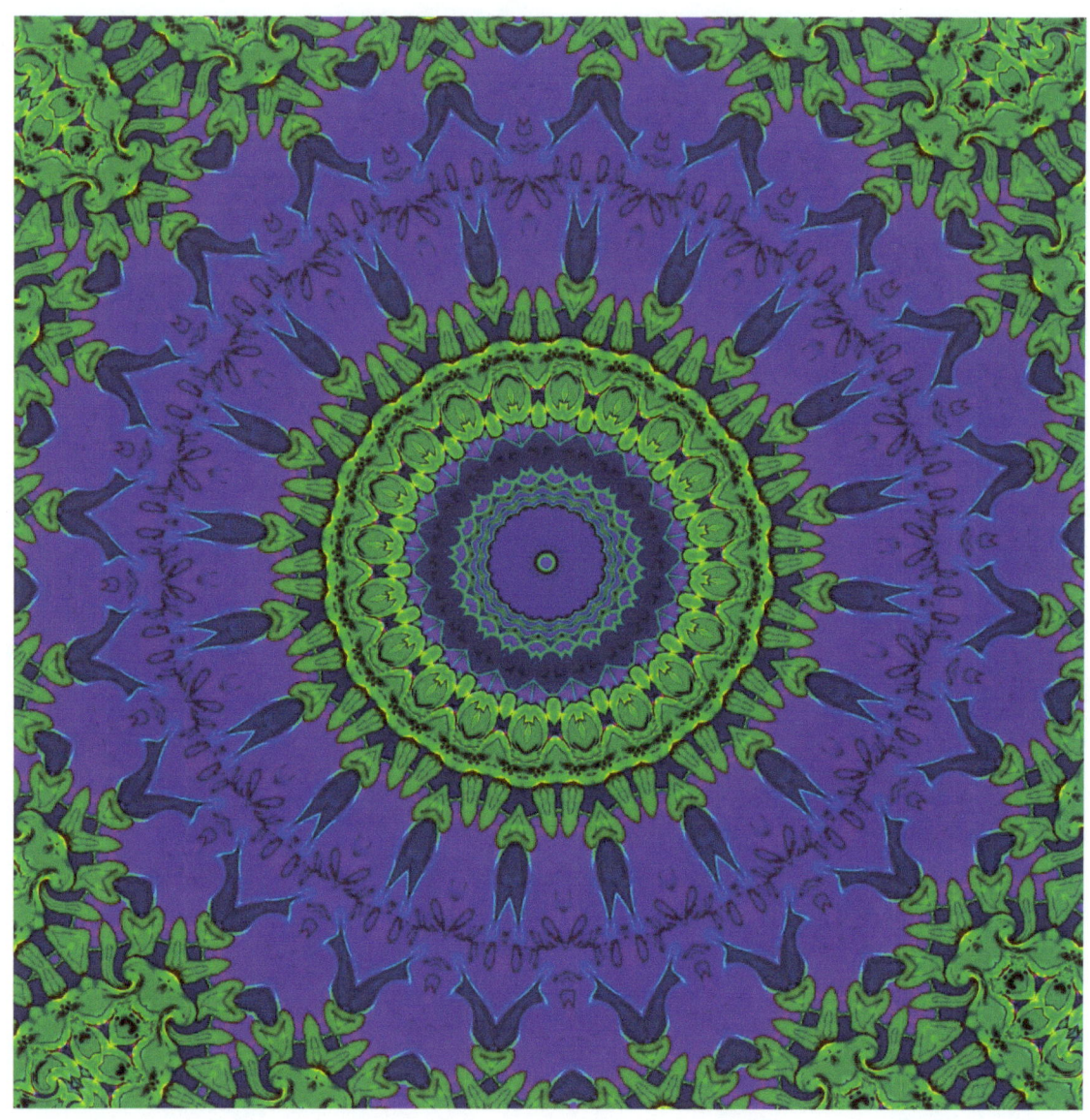

Thank you for purchasing Mandalas in Glorious Color. Check out my other Mandala books 1 through 20. Please go back to where you bought this book and leave feedback.

http://www.GraceBrannigan.com